Longstreet, Stephen,
1907–

A century on wheels

A CENTURY ON WHEELS

The Story of Studebaker

A
CENTURY
ON WHEELS

The Story of Studebaker

A HISTORY, 1852-1952

by

Stephen Longstreet

GREENWOOD PRESS, PUBLISHERS
WESTPORT, CONNECTICUT

This book was catalogued by the Library of Congress as follows:

Longstreet, Stephen, 1907–
    A century on wheels; the story of Studebaker, a history,
1852–1952. Westport, Conn., Greenwood Press, [1970, ᶜ1952]

    xi, 121 p. illus., ports. 23 cm.

    1. Studebaker Corporation.   I. Title.

HD97010.U54S85   1970   70–100238
                        338.7′62′920977289
ISBN 0–8371–3978–3   MARC
Library of Congress   71 [4]

Originally published in 1952 by Henry Holt and Company,
New York

Reprinted with the permission of Studebaker Worthington, Inc.,
New York

Reprinted in 1970 by Greenwood Press, Inc.
51 Riverside Avenue, Westport, CT 06880

Library of Congress catalog card number 70-100238
ISBN 0-8371-3978-3

Printed in the United States of America

10 9 8 7 6 5 4

◄◄◄ *It was the wheel that brought freedom to man, that gave him the road upward, that carried him to cities now dust and gone, that brought him at last to the land to plant and the world to build. Without the wheel the face of the earth would have been empty of man who would have remained crouched in his dark caves away from the sun and joys of existing upright, and not ready to journey to far places . . .*

A *Natural History of the World*
—WILLIAM HERNDON

Acknowledgments

THIS BOOK was written as a popular history for the general reader, so I will not list the hundreds of books or thousands of newspaper files and letters that were turned over to make up a great deal of this volume. But I would like to list in part some acknowledgment of special help.

I want to thank:

Harold S. Vance of The Studebaker Corporation who gave of his time for personal interviews, who let me see their personal files, and who saw that I got the run of the plants at South Bend. My friends at Hill and Knowlton, Inc., who helped in the preparation of this book. The files of the South Bend *Tribune*, the Library of Congress, the New York Public Library, the California State Library, the Placerville *Mountain-Democrat*, the Wells Fargo History Room, the photo collection of the Signal Corps in Washington, and Lt. Commander Montez Tjaden who helped dig out some rare pictures. Geraldine Walters of the Studebaker Library for checking dates, Lura Wallace of the Beverly Hills Public Library for gold rush research and the use of the hall where most of this book was written . . .

And . . .

Four writers and their books that did pioneer work on the subject, whose texts gave me some needed clues: Wells Drury's *To Old Hangtown or Bust* (privately printed in Placerville, California, 1912); Russel Erskine's *History of the Studebaker*

Corporation (1923); Edwin Corle's *John Studebaker* (1948); Smallzried and Roberts' *More Than You Promise* (1942).

And . . .

Files of the New York *Times*, the Los Angeles *Daily News*, the Huntington Library, and the class I taught at the City College of Los Angeles, on whom part of this history was tested while the work was in progress; George Longstreet who helped pick the pictures and gave of his vast knowledge of prints and drawings, and everybody else who helped and can't be listed in this small space.

S. L.

CONTENTS

About the Author

As a writer of the American scene, and an author of books about the development of life in these United States, Stephen Longstreet has been called by *Time* magazine, "the most readable of American writers." With *A Century on Wheels* he brings for the first time to an important industrial subject his knowledge as a novelist, critic, and historian.

Stephen Longstreet's widely diversified career as artist, author, critic, and playwright has included writing and drawing for such magazines as *The New Yorker*, the *Saturday Evening Post*, and *Collier's;* the publication of several novels (*The Pedlocks* and *The Beach House* being the most recent); the production of plays and motion pictures; and a number of one-man shows of his paintings. In 1948 he received the *Billboard* Award for the best play of the year, "High Button Shoes," and the *Photoplay* Gold Medal Gallup Poll Award for the most popular picture of the year, "The Jolson Story." He has received, too, many important awards for his paintings.

Before settling in California, Mr. Longstreet was an avid world traveler, and has recorded some of his adventures in a best seller, *Last Man Around the World.*

Mr. Longstreet teaches a course in Advanced Writing in Los Angeles City College and is a literary critic for the Los Angeles *Daily News.* He and Mrs. Longstreet live in Beverly Hills with their two children.

AN AMERICAN FAMILY

"*Get out and go*" was the motto of the middle of the nineteenth century, and the people were going every chance they had. They went by wagon and they went by horse. The nation was scarred by new-cut roads, by mountain paths through the hostile Rockies, by forest trails newly widened for the wagon trains.

It was a time of Yankee whittlers and emigrant skill. They built the cotton gin and the long Kentuck' rifles that drove the Indians out of the bloody hunting grounds. They held tight to a native way of life with rawhide and hand-hammered steel, with candles molded in pinewood clearings, and they killed the big bear with home-run lead.

It was also a time of get up and do. And the American mechanic was the king pin of the way of life that supplied what was needed and what was wanted: spinning wheels, pick axes, riverboats, boots and saddles, the fringed leather shirts of the mountain men, the new salt-box houses, besides the plow that broke the plains.

There were always the men to make things and the men to buy them. It was a restless and clever age, and no one wanted to die where he had been born, and many wanted a new sun on the horizon every time they woke. It was a time of building of many wheels, of heavy solid wheels of good, seasoned American timbers. Shod with iron hammered onto hickory and oak spokes. And who were these wheel-makers that rolled us in a handful of generations from one great ocean to another? And how did the word Studebaker enter American history?

On February 16, 1852, two young men went into business for themselves in South Bend, Indiana, to shoe horses and repair and build wagons. Their capital, even at a time when the dollar was worth a lot more and lasted longer, was no,t impressive. They had $68, two sets of blacksmith and forge tools. And an idea that in a civilization that depended on horses and wheels for transportation this was a good business for them to be in.

The sign over their shed read:

H & C STUDEBAKER.

Henry was the older of the two brothers but all the Studebaker boys were big and full of muscle, and so Clem was in no sense inferior to his brother in the business of being a smith and wagon-builder.

The morning they opened for business a local man named Harper came in to have two shoes changed on his horse. In half an hour the brothers had heated, shaped, and nailed the new shoes in place. Their price was 25 cents, including the horseshoes. It was the only business they did that day.

Things got even slower, but a few weeks later a Mr. George Earl dropped in and asked if they would build him a wagon. A farm wagon. They built him one in seven days at the price of $175.00. It had straight oak sides, iron hinges, and beautiful wagon wheels with hickory spokes. They painted it green and red. On its sides one of the brothers (no one remembered which one, later) painted in big yellow letters the word: S T U D E B A K E R. Thus was made the first of many million units of transportation to bear the name.

Their first hundred years on wheels had begun . . .

How DID two Studebaker brothers come to open for business in South Bend, and why as smiths and wagon-builders? To know that we must dig out a little of their past, and of the people whose blood ran in their tanned arms and moved their skilled muscles over the white-hot hammered iron.

On September 1, 1736, a battered sailing ship, the *Harle*, made fast to the Market Street wharf of the city of Philadelphia. The ship had sailed from Rotterdam, and her reeking hold held 388 emigrants. The sea-battered trip had taken about ten weeks. The people on board were tired, shabby, and happy to see land. Dysentery, scurvy, and mysterious fevers were the expected events of every sea trip in those days. The *Harle* had gotten more than its share.

Among the passengers who landed were three brothers, who had just managed to scrape together their passage money in Frefeld, Germany. Two had their wives with them. They could speak no English and called themselves Studebecker. They moved on from Philadelphia to Germantown, where land was cheaper and the spaces wider.

Sixty-two years later when recorded history again finds some trace of the family, they had changed the name Studebecker to Studebaker, as being more in the American sound of things. In 1798, court records show that Studebakers were paying taxes in York County. And were already listed as "blacksmiths and woodworkers." They worshiped God as Dunkards and liked such family names as John and Peter and Henry. They had large families, fertile with big sons. They knew no other country as their own.

In 1820 a John Studebaker, aged twenty-one, married a German-American girl from Lancaster, Pennsylvania, named Rebecca Mohler. John wanted elbow room to raise a family and he went from York County to Adams County —a move of a full 30 miles west. John was restless all his life. He settled near a small town named after a local Judge Getty, and called Getty's Town. John built here a brick house and set up as a wagon-builder and blacksmith. He had sons Henry and Clement born in that order. As more Germans settled in the neighborhood, Getty's Town became to be called Gettysburg and that's what it has remained in history.

Thirty-three years later a great battle would be fought here in the hills and along the meadows that the Studebaker boys knew so well. Culp's Hill, Cemetery Ridge, Little Round Top, Spangler's Spring, would echo with war and battle. And engaged on both sides would be wagon trains and gun carriages built by those boys who once ran barefooted on ground to be soaked in blood.

But meantime, the future, as usual to most of us, remained a secret. John Studebaker worked his forge and shoed horses and shaped wagon wheels and worried about the costs (even in those days) of keeping a family going. Andrew Jackson, hero of the battle of New Orleans, was running for election as president of the United States. John Studebaker, a Democrat, told his friends he would vote for "Old Hickory." So would Pennsylvania, so would the whole dang-blasted country. It did. John's third son was born during the Jackson excitement. John Mohler, he was named, born on October 10, 1833. John Mohler was to be the tough one of the litter. He also inherited his father's desire to look on the other side of horizons. Of them all he was to travel the most and adventure in far places, with an eye on the main chance.

Times became hard in the nation, and at Gettysburg as well. Jackson was trying to cut his way through the tariff problem and break the private power of a group that called themselves "The Bank of the United States." There was, of course, talk of inflation; a common cry to the common man in our nation. And then came a panic. John Studebaker felt the hard times, the lean times. Things were not good at the forge. Farmers were not selling their crops, so not shoeing their horses as often or building new wagons. John Studebaker decided to try his luck West.

The West was the great lure, the big number, the special prize waiting some place beyond the Alleghenies for every American. As town life grew crowded, as bad times came, as dullness set in on the fringe of the frontier, the average American packed and went West. Or dreamed about it, if he couldn't pull up stakes, "whistle at the dogs," and start down the rutted road. John Studebaker knew the West as meaning the areas around Ohio and Indiana, and Michigan and Illinois, all called "open country." The real wild West of desert and mountains was for Indians, mountain men, and rattlesnakes. Spain ruled the far western shores . . .

John Studebaker and his sons built themselves a wagon for the trip. We call it today a covered wagon. But in those days it was called a Conestoga wagon, a bear for travel and a devil for taking hard knocks. And it had a whale's belly for what it could swallow in household goods, women, babies, and barnyard truck. The wagon bed was very roomy, the top bows, front and back, bent out, and over all was stretched a canvas duck hood that was supposed to be waterproof, and never was. Actually only the people were waterproof. It took four horses to pull one of these rolling houses on wheels. The details about this wagon are not mere record. The actual wagon still exists today, a prized relic, in the Studebaker museum in South Bend, Indiana.

When John Studebaker stashed away his family, his tools, his wife's spinning wheel, his small livestock, and his stock-in-trade in the wagon, and started West, this wagon was a perfect machine on wheels for travel, and to live in. And not just historical Americana.

History is the recording of the invention or perfection of some weapon and tool that changed nations and social habits. The Studebaker wagon would have died stillborn without the lust for travel of the people of the republic. The proper tool and the one perfect moment in a migratory and virile society had met.

SETTLING AT SOUTH BEND

John Studebaker at first liked the looks of Ohio. It wasn't then what it is today; it was then a land of good standing timber to delight the heart of a wagon man, oak and hickory. And for the family, the loam of fertile clearings to make good fields of wheat, corn, beets, and potatoes. You could still get venison or a squirrel at the price of a well-aimed bullet. Housekeeping was an outdoor baking kiln and heavy iron pots black with many fires. Hard cider, homespun jeans, and lots of hard work colored the frontier. Many men built their wagon sheds first, the houses later.

THE STUDEBAKERS stopped their wagon wheels rolling at Ashland in the north-central part of Ohio. John built a home and a blacksmith shop. Over the door he hung a sign he had burned into a rough-sawed hickory plank with a hot iron. It read: "Owe No Man Anything But to Love One Another." The blacksmith shop and house are no longer standing. But there's a marker five miles east of Ashland, on U.S. Highway 250, where the motto was once plain for all to see in wind and rain and summer heat.

Rebecca cooked, spun, took care of clothes, man, and boys, and had more babies. Two boys and a girl named

Peter, Jacob, and Maria. There was also another panic. This one was called the Panic of 1837. Mr. Martin Van Buren was president now, and he could do very little to help either the nation or the family of the blacksmith.

Here is how a panic works its way down to reach everyone. Three English banks holding notes against American loans failed. The Lancashire cotton mills failed. The cotton ports at New Orleans and along the Mississippi went broke. Crops failed in the Middle West as all prices fell. All this at last caught up the tangled destiny of John Studebaker. He had extended credits, he had signed the notes of friends. And they all went broke together. John sold his property, mortgaged his land to meet his debts and pay off those notes. At forty-eight years of age John Studebaker, with six children to feed, felt he was a failure.

Like most of us, John Studebaker decided maybe he had been voting wrong in the national elections. He bolted his party and voted for "Tippecanoe and Tyler too" — for the "log cabin and the hard cider" party, against what Henry Clay called the "champagne and cake" set in the White House. It didn't help John much in getting over his financial breakdown. No matter how much hot iron he hammered, no matter how many horses he shod, or the number of steel tires he shrank onto hickory wagon wheels, the family were not eating all they should.

The idea of higher education for the children was now only a dream. And John wondered if things wouldn't be better beyond the horizon.

John Studebaker broke down. He gave up swinging the hammer and rode off alone to look over prospects farther West. His oldest son, Henry, now a powerful twenty-two, ran the blacksmith shop, and Clement, seventeen, John Mohler, fifteen, and Peter, twelve, all did their share.

Old John rode on slowly through Ohio and into Indiana. Worried, ailing, hunting in wind and rain and sun for something he had not found in his settling on the frontier in the past. There were many men like John in those days. Men with families who had struggled and lost, and now wandered the wilderness, hoping and looking, desiring and expecting something just a little hard to put into words. They lacked the words, but felt the driving emotion bitterly.

Maybe across the next hill or the one after that they would find *it*.

JOHN STUDEBAKER liked the looks of a town in northern Indiana; it had a river called the St. Joseph; it had a flour mill and lots of cheap water power—a hydraulic works impressive for its day. Maybe this was the place, he felt— the promised land. Maybe here they could settle down and earn their daily bread for sure, and regularly. He rode back home and informed the family of his plans to move. They set to work to sell, and pack, to plan and talk over what they would do or try to do in South Bend.

CLEMENT STUDEBAKER, the second son, couldn't wait for the big move. A year before they were ready to go, he was on his way alone, to prepare the land and the place for the family. And also, he wanted to see the country, lots of it. Clement traveled by way of Sandusky, Ohio, then by boat to a place, still not impressive, called Detroit, in Michigan. At Niles, Michigan, he got onto a stagecoach and in the heat of dusty summer crossed the Michigan-Indiana line and got to South Bend. He was nineteen, but didn't think of himself as a boy.

Clem was impressed, even by the muddy streets, the board sidewalks, the iron hitching posts, the speed of the local buggies. He took in the whole country. At nearby Mishawaka was the Milburn wagon factory, and an iron works. There was even talk of a railroad to connect

Chicago and the East. And its silver rails, its chugging, high-nosed engines, would pass through South Bend.

At first Clem worked in the Eliakim Briggs Threshing Machine Works, for 50 cents a day. There was an opening for a schoolteacher, and in those days college degrees and such nonsense weren't part of frontier education. Any man who could read, cipher a bit, and write fairly well could teach school. Clem did. He took an interest in the town and a year later watched the first train come through with fireworks, speeches, and free deer barbecue. There was also square dancing to a fancy fiddle. Clem helped stomp the place down.

In the fall of 1851, Old John and his family decided to trust their old covered wagon rather than the new railroad and came to South Bend to join Clem. Old John was a worn-out man now, and the burden of support of the family rested on the strong shoulders of his sons.

Clem was not too impressed with the future of schoolteaching. Henry was blacksmithing again, but for pay for others. The two brothers talked it over and determined to go into business for themselves. Their capital was $68, and after they set up a shop, even less. And so, as related in our opening pages, on February 16, 1852, the firm of H. & C. Studebaker opened for business.

They shod horses and remembered with pleasure the wagon they had built for George Earl, which they had lettered in yellow paint as the first S T U D E B A K E R wagon by the new firm. But they did not find any real rush for their skill in wagon-building. The only other wagon customer that year was a Mrs. Stover, a widow rich only in fatherless children. She needed a wagon to haul farm crops to the markets. The brothers built her the farm wagon, but it is to be doubted if they ever got any cash for it. Most likely only farm products, hams, and a few sides of beef if the slaughtering season was close.

WITH NO RUSH for wagons, the brothers shod horses, repaired rifles, made candlesticks, hammered out solid door
hinges and locks for farmhouses and barns. But they kept
their trust in the moving wheels, the long wagon trains
passing their doors, moving West . . .

WHEN THERE WAS no iron work to do, John Mohler, a good
son, got up at four in the morning and cut two cords of
wood in the forest and he and his father peddled them in
town for four dollars. The money went to pay for food
and blue jeans and seed for the growing family and their
needs. There was nothing shameful in cutting wood and
peddling it in the streets. But it was looked down upon by
some as a sign of frontier failure to make a farm pay or a
business go. Or that one lacked the skill and knack to make
a go of tanning, or manufacturing, or cotton factoring, or
even of a hotel or the cattle business.

Almost a decade later another shabby man, driving
a light Studebaker farm wagon, would be seen along the
streets of an Illinois town, his little son at his side, a load
of firewood in the wagon bed. A shabby man in an old
army overcoat, smelling of whisky and defeat and poverty.

People would point him out and say, "There goes
Sam Grant, used to be in the army and the Mexican War.
But got chucked out for his drinking. A no-good. Failed
in everything. Never amount to anything . . ."

THREE

A YOUNG MAN GOES WEST

Hangtown Gals are lovely creatures
Think they'll marry Mormon preachers
Heads thrown back to show their features
Ha! Ha! Ha! Hangtown Gals!

To church they very seldom venture
Hoops so large they can not enter
Go it, Gals! You're young and tender!
Shun the pick-and-shovel gender!
— GOLD RUSH SONG

Young John Mohler Studebaker was feeling the itch for travel in his feet. Like Old John, his father, horizons were calling him. Since 1849 the gold rush to California had changed the pulse beat of the country. Wagon trains passed every day through South Bend, and tall tales filled the newspapers of solid gold nuggets "big as hen's eggs" you found by just shaking them out of the grass roots. Almost everyone it seemed was going some place, following the advice of a man called Horace Greeley, who had just said "Go West, young man!" while he himself stayed in New York City and ran a newspaper.

You took a pack and you walked, or you pushed a wheelbarrow, or you got a covered wagon, and some bacon and beans and cleared out. You took along a pick and shovel (and some stout bags for the gold, naturally) and you went. If you had the cash you traveled in style, the long way around the Horn, by clipper ship, or across Panama, where if you were lucky the fever and Indians didn't get you. There was no lost generation: they were on their way West to dig gold.

For John Mohler—his mind made up—there was naturally only one way to go. By wagon. The thing to do was to find a big party who would take him along in return for a spanking new Studebaker wagon, built by himself and his brothers. In 1853 John Mohler made a deal with a passing wagon train. In return for a new wagon they would take him across to California and, as he liked to eat, give him three square meals a day. The boys built the wagon in ten days. A good one with extra large wheels for new paths West, and Clem did the iron work, standing in smoke and heat, driving the power and shape into the iron for the Studebaker wagon to cross the Great Divide— the tall Rockies, the high timber, the tracks of eagles.

John Mohler was six feet tall, most all of it muscle, and the beginning of a good tough beard. One hundred and ninety pounds, brown-haired, and blue-eyed, and aching to go. His mother sewed $65 into a belt, and gave him a Bible and three suits of clothes she had spun and made. He was ready for El Dorado, his only worry being: *was* the belt big enough to carry back all the gold he would find in California?

THEY MOVED West slowly, repairing, hunting, and exploring the roads and trails ahead. John worked hard. He helped break camp and herd the horses and oxen. He harnessed and drove, and when off duty walked alongside of the groaning wagons. He helped build campfires and gather the wagons into a great protecting circle every night. They went slowly through timber and through tall grass, and saw for the first time the huge plains, endless before them.

They had long since passed through the new town of Chicago, raw, dirty, and busy slaughtering hogs, shipping buffalo robes, hunting a dollar, and moving freight and lake shipping. They went past Council Bluffs, Iowa, and John saw the sod huts, the black loam of first plowings, the immense skies of the outer frontier. Green corn and wheat appeared and ahead they talked of meeting mountains with snow on them all year around. And deserts where not a drop of water had ever existed. Hostile Indians, painted and cruel. And there was campfire talk of wagon trains snowed in, like the Donner Party, and the horror when they ate each other. Only the mountain men with the party nodded at each other and grinned and said, "meat's meat."

It was at Council Bluffs that John played his first and last hand of three-card monte . . . and lost everything almost but his shirt and 50 cents. It was good to get out, way out, where space seemed never to stop and where the river crossings cooled one off and sudden storms tore at men and wagons and cattle went insane with fear. It was tough going . . .

The wagon train was torn and tattered now. The wagons broken and repaired, the canvases faded and patched. Even the people looked worn and weather-stained. But they made it. They aimed at Hangtown, their destination. Every train in those years had a wagon with a sign on it: CALIFORNY OR BUST! We don't know if it was John's wagon, or rather the wagon that John traded for the trip.

Hangtown was not much on the eyes, they heard. A clutter of shacks in a deep clearing among the evergreens. A mountain camp, a mining town, rough, ready, and mean.

Rude paths served for streets and the Empire Saloon (rumor was it had the *only* coat of paint in town) served a raw whisky at a dollar a shot. Small change wasn't considered legal tender in mining camps. All deals cash, you paid or starved — or worse, went thirsty.

How did all this impress John Mohler? We know because he left a full record. It's in a rare document called *To Old Hangtown or Bust*, paperbound. Printed for Private Circulation, Placerville (formerly Hangtown), California, 1912. In it we don't find much about the trip itself. How the wagon train climbed up the eastern slope of the Sierras south of Lake Tahoe to come at last into California. They couldn't believe it at first, but they went on going slowly, through Desolation Valley, Strawberry Flat, and climbing down the western slope, carried on now by the idea they were close to their journey's end. It was on August 31, 1853, that John Mohler's wagon train came to Hangtown, known by people who wrote letters back home by its post office name of Old Dry Diggins.

Maybe John Mohler wasn't impressed, but he was excited. It was like a thousand other mining towns, all created because in 1848, at Sutter's Saw Mill, on the South Fork of the American River, a drifting jack-of-all-trades, one James W. Marshall, building a sawmill for John August Sutter, found some yellow flakes glittering in the tail race of the mill run. "GOLD!"

Old Dry Diggins had a shifty, shifting population of about 2,000 when John got there. And an oak tree from which several men had been hanged for robbery or rape (or some other vague idea) by the "law-and-order" element that decided they would look better dead. Mob justice and vigilante procedure were quick. They hung so many some said it only seemed proper to call Old Dry Diggins, Hangtown.

LIFE IN THE GOLD FIELDS

This seems a good place to quote John Mohler's actual words. It's rare enough that one finds a maker of history also a historian. It got better every time he told it. He enjoyed telling it—his way.

We were more than five months on the road, and landed in California in August, 1853, and I had but fifty cents in my pocket.

Of course a big crowd gathered around us, and while we were trying to get them to talk about the gold mines they insisted on asking questions about what had happened in the States since they had heard from their friends. While the hubbub was going on a man came up and asked if there was a wagon-maker in the crowd of new arrivals. They pointed me out and he asked: "Are you a wagon-maker?"

"Yes sir," I answered, as big as life, with my 50-cent piece in my pocket.

The man was "Joe" Hinds. He offered me a job in his shop, but I replied that I came to California to mine for gold and that I had never thought of taking any other kind of a job. Hinds turned on his heel and walked off. He was a man of few words.

After he was gone a man, whom I afterwards found out was Dr. Worthem, stepped up and very politely said:

"Will you let me give you a little advice, young man?" I said yes, and he continued: "Take that job and take it quick."

His manner impressed me. He said that there would be plenty of time to dig gold, which was not always a sure thing, and that the job just offered me was a mighty fine chance for a stranger.

I thought it was a pretty good idea, and as there was four of us youngsters who had come together, and all of us were broke, I decided to go to work for the wagon-maker if he would take me.

I followed Hinds to his shop. It was above Stony Point, I remember, and was a log house, with the back wall made by digging into the hill. There were coffee-sack bunks in which we slept, and in the middle of the room was a sheet iron stove on which the cooking was done.

I explained that I had decided to see what he wanted me to do, and he said he wanted me to make wheelbarrows for the miners. He wanted 25 and would pay me $10 apiece. So I began the next morning. The tools were the worst you ever saw, and the only material was pitch-pine lumber. I got along very slow at first, and at noon found that I was hungry. So I went down to the square where there was a tent with a big sign, "Philadelphia Hotel." The rule then was to pay a dollar before you went in. But I had no dollar. And my three companions were in the same fix. In talking with Simons, the proprietor, I told him I was from South Bend, Indiana, and found that he was from a place nearby. He was Dutch, and I talked some of my Pennsylvania Dutch to him. Finally, after I told him that I was working for Hinds, he let us go in, and we ate enough for three days.

Simons went over to find out from Hinds if we were lying, and he had plenty of time, we stayed so long at the table. The other boys were wild to get started at mining, so I took them over to Hinds and got him to trust them for pick and shovel and pan.

At the end of the second day I got one wheelbarrow

done. Hinds looked at it. "What do you call that?" he asked, puffing his old pipe.

"I call it a wheelbarrow," I answered.

"A hell of a wheelbarrow," was the comment. And he was correct, for as a matter of fact the wheel was a little crooked. But I put up the best excuse I could.

"You asked me if I was a wagon-maker and I said I was. I didn't say that I was a wheelbarrow-maker and I think I can do better on the next one." I got myself provided with better tools and turned out a fair product, making a wheelbarrow a day.

Hundreds and thousands who tried the mines never made a success. But we who stuck to steady jobs at good wages and saved our money were sure of doing well. Joe Hinds and I worked many a night all night—he making new picks and I repairing stages that came in late and that had to get out at 6 o'clock in the morning. It was not always the fault of the mines, however, that the young fellows failed to make a stake, for they gambled away their gold dust like so many reckless sports that they were.

He tells us one of his own "reckless" adventures:

When the Adams Express Company failed I had $3000 in the bank—all the money I had in the world. Hinds, my partner, had $22,000 in the same bank. I remember that it was 2 o'clock in the afternoon that the bank was closed, and we all knew that if it didn't open the next morning the boys would come in and tear up everything, provided they thought there was any money in the place. That's where Hinds and his level head came in. He knew that the express people would try to get their money out that night, for the failure was caused by lack of money elsewhere, and not at Hangtown. You all remember that the bank backed right up against Hangtown Creek, and without saying a word to anybody Hinds made up his plan. He hid in the brush back of the bank just across the creek, and watched.

Sure enough, just as he expected, he saw the express people creep out of the building at about 2 o'clock in the morning with the bags of gold. He trailed them and saw them put the money in old Joe Douglas' safe. The rest was easy for Hinds. He waked me up and told me what had been done, and said he was going to levy an attachment on the safe, and from what he saw he was confident there was enough to pay us both, so he asked me if I wanted to stand in on the attachment suit. Of course I did, and we got out the papers bright and early. You can depend on it we didn't waste any time. Douglas, the old sinner, denied that the money was in his safe, but the officer found it and served the attachment, and as there was no defense we got the coin in short order, every dollar of it, while hundreds of others, after long waiting, received only 15 to 30 per cent. Hinds threw that money into a wheelbarrow and trundled it through the streets of Hangtown.

Like many other Americans of his time, John Mohler's hard-earned cash was to found something so big, so important to the progress of his country, that he would have thought it the cockeyed vision of a fortuneteller primed on 40-rod whisky if he could have seen to what use his saved money would be put.

HOME TO BUSINESS

John Mohler Studebaker was in Hangtown from 1853 to 1858. He came there a trusting boy of nineteen and left it a tough, successful man of twenty-four. He saw the hard life and the cruelty. There is evidence he watched the hanging at nearby Coloma of a Dr. Crane, and one Mickey Free. The fire department and band of Hangtown, of which John was a member, played theme music for the double hanging.

BUT LIFE WASN'T always exciting. Mining life was back-breaking work. John made wheelbarrows, pick axes, repaired stagecoaches, shod horses, and repaired harnesses. And he saved his money. By 1855 John had $3,000 stashed away. He no longer trusted banks or express companies. His wheelbarrows of green pitch pine were needed and he began to be known as "Wheelbarrow Johnny." Today the Placerville Chamber of Commerce has one of these wheelbarrows in its local museum.

BY 1856 a postmaster named Nugent had made the town fairly respectable (after a long fight) and it was now legally Placerville. Only some of the citizens didn't know it. When the hanging oak was cut down—a sad day—a saloon called "The Hangman's Tree Bar" was put up to respectfully mark the spot.

John Mohler was one of the solid characters of the town. Phil Armour had opened a butcher shop, and Mark Hopkins sold garden vegetables, and "fresh eggs" that had come around the Horn, at three dollars each. The future packing-house and railroad kings and the future wagon- and auto-maker were just young men on the make in Placerville. All under twenty-five.

John might have stayed on in California, but for the letters from home. H. & C. Studebaker were still in business, but finding it rough going. They lacked capital, and all they could turn out with their own limited resources was a dozen or so Studebaker wagons a year. They believed in their wagons, in the future growth of transportation. But without capital they'd never make many more wagons a year in their own way; making them only on order, buying material when they could pay for it.

John Mohler out in California also believed in the future of transportation in a growing nation. Even here in Placerville the big world came in on wheels. Look at the local playbills. Lotta Crabtree and Lola Montez, the dancer, whose every wriggle drove the miners at the Palace into cheers. Adah Menken, who, bound nudely (but respectably in tights) onto the back of a wild horse in *Mazeppa*, was daring and satisfying for those who didn't care for Edwin Booth or Yankee Sullivan, the prize fighter. The express companies, with hard notorious killers "riding shotgun," connected the towns to Frisco and the world with their rushing wheels. Later the stagecoaches, with Bret Harte or Mark Twain bouncing on their dusty cushions went every place a four- or six-horse team could climb. Yes, John believed in the future of transportation.

He had $8,000 now, in gold, coin, and nuggets in his money belt. He'd go home and put money into wagons and wheels with his brothers.

If they could, he figured, build 200, even 300 wagons a year there would still be a shortage of transportation in a growing country. So in April, 1858, John left Placerville for home. He had a last drink with the boys at the Golden Nugget saloon, including his comrades of *Old Confidence,* the fire-fighting machine he had helped push through the streets the night the whole town almost went up in flames.

The gold belt was tight around his waist, he had $200 set aside in a pocket for traveling expenses, and the coach for Sacramento was waiting in the square. Bottoms up, boys . . .

It took 21 days to reach Taboga Island from which one could see the pirate-raided port of Panama and the start of the railroad East across the Isthmus. John crossed the continent in four and a half hours by rail. It was his first railroad ride. He was most impressed with a wheel. The big driving wheel of the locomotive. He knew wheels, and the steel wheel was a good one. At the Atlantic side he took passage in the one-funneled steamer *George Law,* a swift packet under Captain Edward R. Slocum. He was restless now to get home to South Bend. He stood at the rail as the *George Law* passed Sandy Hook and went up the Narrows to dock at Warren Street. New York was the biggest town in the nation, and John was impressed. He took it all in, particularly the many fine carriages on the avenues, the sleek horses, the polished harnesses, the fine people who sat back and were transported around Central Park, down the tree-shaded streets to the station of the steam cars. He hadn't believed there could be that many wheels in the world. And New York was only one city.

John was five days in New York, then took Commodore Vanderbilt's cars on the New York Central to South Bend, a journey of a day and a half. Past ripe fields, fine houses, and pikes and roads dusty with the traffic of wheels moving along the rolling prairie by the shores of Lake Erie. John sat in the car, the money belt comfortable against his skin and he felt happy at going home. Home, the poet was to say, is where you go, and they have to let you in. He knew he would be more than welcome.

He suspected now that the gold from California's streams and hills had enriched the nation, and that which found its way in the hands of the men like himself would grow a thousandfold if it were pumped into the economic life-stream of the growing, expanding nation. Sure — why not, asked John Mohler Studebaker, would-be gold miner, successful smith and wheelbarrow-maker, going home to become a businessman . . . a new, and increasingly important kind of an American.

THE WAGON-MAKERS

A tight-knit family, the Studebakers, and they were happy to get letters that John Mohler was coming home. The years had been busy ones for them, too. Jacob, the baby of the family, at eight years of age had gone into business selling and trading marbles, taffy, and forge scraps. At seventeen, Peter was a store clerk, earning his $15 a month and not liking it. He saved up $100, had his brothers make him a peddler's cart, and loaded it with such notions as tin pans, matches, pins, needles, knives, scissors, wax, and flatirons and went out to tempt the farm wives with glitter and clatter. It didn't make him rich, so he went into business with a brother-in-law, at Goshen, Indiana, dealing in general merchandise: nails, leather, horse collars, glass, shoes, and cheese.

AT THE FIRM of H. & C. Studebaker, there was progress of a kind. The forge managed to keep noisy and busy. In 1857 Henry and Clem built a carriage, their first, and everyone said it was a dandy. Fancy hand-worked iron trim, the kind of courting buggy any boy and girl would be proud to be seen in — heading for the nearest shady lane to spoon. The brothers lacked capital to expand. But now and then they ran into a bit of luck. There had been the time when supply wagons, several hundred of them, for the U.S. Army's frontier stations were ordered from the Mishawaka Wagon Works near South Bend. George Milburn, owner of the plant, could fill part of the order, and he called in the Studebaker brothers and asked them if they could build him 100 army wagons according to Washington specifications, in six months.

Henry and Clem cheerfully said, "Of course, Mr. Milburn," and signed the contracts after nodding their heads. Back in the shop they weren't so sure. How were they going to build 100 army-designed wagons in six months in their small shop? Skilled wagon-builders, seasoned timber were lacking. It took three years to season good wagon timber properly. They solved that problem by building a drying kiln, their own invention, and drying green timbers swiftly. This process was part of their plant for many years. They hired men and trained them quickly. Put up sheds, added forges, and began to shape wheels. Parts they couldn't produce they farmed out to a tool company to make for them. The hundred army wagons were ready in 90 days, three months before their contracts called for delivery.

Clem and Henry were now men who had tasted the full red meat of mass production for the first time and they wanted more. If they could only keep their wagon sheds and forges going, not falling back to a dozen wagons a year. But while they had delivered their hundred wagons they had not made too much on the deal. They still needed real cash capital, and now John was on his way home with California gold. They would make wagons now, not as contractors to another wagon firm, but as their own wagons on which they could paint their own name, S T U - D E B A K E R, in yellow paint.

John Mohler came home stuffed with ideas. In June, 1858, the reunited brothers held a meeting at H & C S T U -

DEBAKER and listened to John. Henry was now thirty-one, Clem twenty-six. John the wanderer, twenty-four, had traveled far, and he had visions and memories beyond the daily routine of South Bend and just a small wagon shop. John talked of the West, of New York, of the busy roads of the nation he had seen. Now was the time to take risks, expand. But Henry was tired of the business. He wanted to farm. The risks of expanding were not for him. So John Mohler bought out his brother Henry's right in the firm. With the rest of his money he and Clem recapitalized the firm with them as the sole two partners. The money belt was empty but their hopes were high.

JOHN MOHLER — to be known among his friends and in the business from now on as just J.M. — believed in advertising. Not just painting a firm name on a barn. But real advertising, in newspapers. And so, just after the new partnership was formed a local South Bend paper carried John's first ad:

> *Encourage Home Industry*
> *Northern Indiana*
> *Carriage and Wagon Factory*
>
> **H. & C. STUDEBAKER**
>
> Would call attention of the public to their large and splendid assortment of Carriages, Buggies, Wagons and Sleigh-cutters. They can now assure the public that the work in their establishment cannot be excelled in Northern Indiana for durability or fineness of finish. None but the best workmen are employed in the Factory, consequently it is the only establishment in this part of Indiana that will warrant their work. Blacksmithing, painting, trimming, custom work, and repair done on short notice in the best style. The new brick factory is on Michigan Street south of the American Hotel.

EIGHTEEN HUNDRED AND SIXTY was a year that rocked the nation, and there was excitement in the wagon-building clan of Studebaker, too. A brand new party called the Republicans was running a long, lean, backwoods lawyer for president of the United States. He only got 40 per cent of the votes. But that was enough to set Abe Lincoln's tall body in the White House rocking chair, for the rest of the votes were divided among the three other opposing candidates.

It was with a feeling that change was not for them, and that their way of life was their own, that the people of the South threatened to leave the Union. The dark, lean man, Lincoln, said he was going to support the Union with force if he had to.

THE BIGGEST family event that year in South Bend was the marriage of John Mohler. He fell in love and soon brought things to a climax. The girl was fair-haired Mary Jane Stull, of German ancestry, but of American upbringing. She was a farmer's daughter and lived on a farm with a huge white house, about ten miles west of South Bend. John drove out there one day to sell a wagon to her father, Henry Stull, and saw Mary. He first sold the wagon, then came back and courted Mary.

The Stulls were well off. They had made a good farm of their place and respected God for his bounty and his mercies as good Dunkards. Dunkardism was a simple faith, and John was part of it and while it had its limits, it had a grace and a purity for simple, hard-working people. When Henry Stull earnestly asked John if he believed in miracles, John looked at Mary and said drily, "Yes, I've experienced one."

THE WEDDING took place in the packed white Stull farmhouse (both families had been large and fertile) on January 3, 1860. Elder David Miller performed the wedding services while a heavy Indiana snowstorm beat against the windows. There was three feet of snow on the roads. John and Mary had planned a wedding trip to Chicago. After the last shouting toast and the last wet kisses, and some gay advice, John and Mary got into Mr. Stull's best sleigh to be driven to the New York Central station at La Porte. A Chicago train would be flagged down for them. The storm grew worse.

The railroad depot was just a freezing shed. The bride and groom stamped their chilling feet and rubbed their red noses and were informed that the Chicago train was snowbound up the line and would be more than six hours late. A train appeared out of the mist of snow and sleet and John and Mary got in and huddled around the red-hot stove with which coaches were heated in those days. It didn't matter that the train was going in the wrong direction, away from Chicago. Freezing to death was no way to start a honeymoon. The train was going through South Bend, Elkhart, and Goshen. And they decided to get off at Goshen where John's brother, Peter, ran a general store. They stayed a week with Peter. J.M. was impressed with Peter's business methods.

It was while honeymooning at Peter's that John Mohler put a proposition to his brother. Peter was a good salesman. Why not make his store an out-of-town sales-room for Studebaker wagons? Peter said he didn't have room for wagons among the hung hams and tin pans and flour sacks and cracker barrels.

"Build some sheds," John said.

"That would cost money . . . all of five dollars," Peter said.

"Go ahead."

So the salesroom of three stalls, or "repository" as the brothers called it, was built in the spring. Peter's ideas of costs were right. It cost about five dollars. So Stude-baker had its first out-of-town salesroom, and shiny new wagons were sold from it as soon as they were delivered. Peter asked for more and got them.

Wagons were the magic carpets of the people. There were vast lands opening up to homesteaders — men and their families were being moved into the new federal lands — for as voters and citizens of soon-to-be states, they would vote the way a land-giving administration would like. It was a pattern to be used a lot, later in our history — but it increased the sales of wagons then — and turned the wilderness into farms.

JOHN M. HAD a flair for creating forceful advertising copy. For its day, it was more than daring; lots of people considered it a foolish waste of good money.

The ad read:

Common Sense

If you set out to buy a horse, you don't deliberately take chances on a spavined, wind-broken, moon-eyed, knock-kneed animal. What you seek for is a beast that is sound, strong, handsome and enduring. You don't buy a horse simply because the price is the lowest. But how is it when you buy a Wagon or Carriage? Are you particular to get a vehicle that you know to be, in workmanship, beauty and strength, the best in the market? Or do you take something made up of culled lumber, inferior iron, unskilled labor, and worthless paints and varnishes, simply because the price is low, and for the time being it can pass muster in appearance, forgetting the hazard to yourself and family involved in riding in such a conveyance?

If you want a FARM WAGON, FREIGHT WAGON, SPRING WAGON, PHAETON, OPEN BUGGY, TOP CARRIAGE, LANDAU or vehicle of any kind, see that it bears the name "STUDEBAKER" which is a certain guaranty of excellence and superiority.

When wanting anything in this line be sure to call on

H & C STUDEBAKER.

JOHN MOHLER didn't wait for customers to come on in. When the new brick factory had a half-dozen gleaming wagons finished he and Old John, his father, would drive the string out into the country and sell them direct to the farmers. The wagons were now painted red, green, and yellow, and the name: S T U D E B A K E R was lettered in a dignified and easy-to-read, rich black.

When money was hard to get they took in trade farm crops, pigs, apples, whatever the farmer wanted to trade for the wagons. In town they sold these products for cash, if they could. Or—ate it. But the main thing, as J.M. saw it, was to get their wagons around. The product would create its own demand once people saw how good a wagon they made.

J.M. was a shrewd, crossroads corner trader. He knew how much to ask, how to barter and trade so that each side seemed to have the advantage. He did pretty well. Not that they weren't fooled once in a while. The family told the story for years about a handsome bay gelding with big, brown beautiful eyes that J.M. traded for a fine new wagon. It was a smart-looking horse—only it couldn't keep to the road. It was stone blind. Some Yankee horse trader had done J.M. out of a good wagon. J.M. didn't let on he had been stung, and sold the horse to their best salesman, his brother Peter. There is no record of what Peter did with the blind gelding. But no one thinks he kept it long.

THE FIRM was growing. By the end of 1860 they had a manufacturing shop, a paint room, a lumber yard of their own, an office (not too fancy), and Peter's out-of-town showroom. The firm employed 14 workmen, not counting the hard-working brothers themselves. They knew good wood, they seasoned and dried their timber, they bought raw iron and hammered it into wagon shapes on their own forges. They sewed wagontops, greased axles, and took pride in the good colors and good paint with which they finished off their wagons. J.M. was a fine wheel striper, an art in those days. It took real skill to spin the wheel and get just the right thin line of red or blue or white paint into the wheel rim and hub.

THE BROTHERS cheerfully estimated their business as worth the full sum of $10,000. Not that anyone offered them that much for the wagon works. Not that they would have sold it. They just liked to have a good round figure of what they thought they were worth, and $10,000 seemed a neat, solid sum. Involved scientific bookkeeping was not part of the early struggle of the American success story. A lot of inventory and figures could be carried in a well-stocked mind, John Mohler always felt.

AND SO DEDICATED

The roaring destiny of America was reaching the boiling point and was about to explode with a roar of blood and fire. The trouble had been a long time coming and the fuel of conflict was well stacked and inflammable. Speaking to the South in his Inaugural Address on March 4, 1861, President Lincoln said:

> In your hands, my dissatisfied fellow countrymen, and not mine, are the momentous issues of civil war . . . You can have no conflict without being yourselves the aggressors. We must not be enemies.

Two days later the Studebakers read in the South Bend newspapers that Jefferson Davis, president of the "Confederate States of America," had called for 100,000 Southern volunteers. John said war was coming. Peter said it would only last two months.

On April 12, shore batteries — once Union property — began firing on ships trying to relieve Fort Sumter in Charleston Harbor. The South had fired the first shot. Three days later Lincoln called for 75,000 volunteers to preserve the Union. Farm boys and clerks marched out singing "We Are Coming, Father Abraham." Robert E.

Lee declined the offer of Commander-in-Chief of the Union Armies, deciding he belonged to Virginia.

A shabby man, driving a Studebaker farm wagon loaded with firewood, got off and offered his services to the Union to drill local volunteers. U.S. Grant had no uniform, no horse, no sword. He drilled his men in his wood-cutting clothes. And in the South the farmers went for their rifles singing it was "a rich man's war — and a poor man's fight."

The Studebakers were Dunkards, a religion of brotherly love that saw war as evil, and only evil. As the young men poured into the armies, the Studebaker brothers wondered what the future held for them. They were too old mostly for active service. Only young men and boys could fight the bitter wars of the Virginia muds, slog along the Mississippi, and charge briskly at Bull Run, Cold Harbor, and march against rebel yells into the Wilderness. Henry was thirty-five and ailing. Clem was thirty ("Ten years younger, and I'd enlist"). John Mohler was twenty-eight. Old John, sixty-two, was steeped in Dunkardism and he refused to let Jacob, seventeen, join the army.

The Union armies were badly in need of modern supplies for making war. They had been fighting piddling wars on a dozen Indian frontiers, with mounted men and carbines and some light cannon. But this was to be a real war of massed armies led by some of the greatest military minds the world had yet seen. Grant, Lee, Jackson, Sheridan, Sherman, Longstreet, Meade. And such glory-hunters as Custer, Hampton, J.E.B. (only Yankees called him "Jeb") Stuart. The armies were still using materials left over from the Mexican War, and the factories of the North had to be put swiftly into operation to turn out the stuff that armies fought with, moved with, and used to win battles.

In 1862, military purchasing agents from Washington came to South Bend to look over the firm of H. & C. Studebaker. They asked how many wagons the brothers could turn out in a month, three months, six months, a year. They signed their first big government contract for wagons, gun caissons, meat and ammunition wagons. They even made a beer wagon to deliver lager to German troops who had been promised beer in battle.

They had to expand, and at once. Shops and sheds were enlarged, bigger forges built. New land was bought and new buildings put up and new equipment put in. Peter came back into the plant to work. And over all a new sign went up:

STUDEBAKER BROTHERS

IN PENNSYLVANIA they had been drilling for oil. Near Tarentum rock oil had been found in old salt wells. Colonel Edwin L. Drake bravely began to drill and at the extraordinary depth of 69 feet brought in a 40-barrel well! By 1862 a real oil boom was in progress. Seven hundred fifty-nine thousand barrels of oil were shipped for the war effort at a cost of $18 million. Studebaker wagons carted a lot of this oil to army camps and cities under fire.

WHILE THE WAR went on and grew every day more bloody, the nation grew faster and faster. What had been a farming nation, J.M. saw, of the second class, took on new, world stature. We almost went to war with England over the stopping of our ships. And American farmers fed not only the armies in the field but Europe, too. In 1860, '61, and '62 the harvests failed in Europe. Hogs and corn and wheat were exported and paid for by a third of a billion dollars. Wagons loaded with these products poured huge cargoes into the holds of Europe-bound ships. America, by some paradox, was becoming a world power, while at home it beat itself to its knees in a war of brother against brother.

WITH FAMINE in Europe the seaports were sucking in dis-
placed persons. Lincoln approved a bill permitting factories
to bring in working men from Europe. And to give all men
breathing space more of the western territories were
opened under free homestead provisions. Whole wilder-
nesses were colonized by Union men and their families to
make loyal Northern states. And all this took transportation never dreamed of ten years before. Wagons and horses
moved the war and moved the settlers, the imported
factory workers, and their families. Daring rebel raiders
might cut the rail lines, burn ships, but wagons could be
replaced, wheels repaired. New roads were built and the
factories could not keep up with the demand for finished
products.

Armour, Pillsbury, McCormick, were expanding
meat-packing, flour-milling, and farm machinery. Cattle,
coal, wheat, had to be moved. And the war went on. It
was focused in 1863 on Grant who had battered the Southern forces to bits in the West and at Vicksburg. And on
the farmland around a village called Gettysburg, where
Old John Studebaker had once had a forge, and where his
older sons still remembered the peach orchards and pike
roads and summer heat on the ridges and country lanes,
there was to be fought the deciding battle. If Lee shattered
the Union armies and took Washington from the rear,
Lincoln would perhaps have to make a peace and split the
Union.

IN THE private collection of a Southern family, in New
Orleans, there still exists a bundle of old letters, written
by a young soldier who came north with Lee to invade.
In one letter are the lines

. . . we have burned parts of Chambersburg and robbed
the bank there. But best of all we captured a lot of blankets

and food . . . sixteen Studebaker wagons into which we put part of our powder train. It's summer and hot and the fruit is green. The farmers are well off and we shall be in Washington in a week at the most . . .

But Heath, one of Lee's men, had heard there was a shoe factory at Gettysburg and he begged permission to go with men and wagons and get shoes on his men. The captured wagons lined the pike road and the greatest battle ever fought on American earth was joined.

On the third day the battle ended in the rain.

The countercharge of Webb's Pennsylvanians went past in a blur of fury. Went past, and sent the last shots into the patched buttocks of homespun pants. The blood haze that would be Lincoln's Gettysburg ended in a blast of bugle-ringing charges. The day died away *de crescendo*. And many a wounded man escaped in Lee's retreat in one of the captured wagons. For days the wagon trains moved South carrying back to their native soil the remains of a lost but gallant cause.

AND WHEN the Union soldiers went home as the war ended — many of them were rewarded by free land in the West. One of great ports into the seas of the free land was St. Joseph, Missouri. Here the homesteaders outfitted and looked over the wagon market.

EIGHT

THE WHEELS SPIN

Postwar expansion rode mostly on wagon wheels . . .

> I, Peter Studebaker, agree to sell all the wagons
> my brother Clem can make.
>   (signed) *Peter Studebaker*

> I agree to make all he can sell.
>   (signed) *Clem Studebaker*

Peter Studebaker was a salesman, one of the first of
the great drummers-up of business in a nation that was
going to be famous for its salesmanship. Peter did not stay
in South Bend and dream. He toured the nation. No town
was too small to see the well-dressed, prosperous, smiling,
cheerful Peter Studebaker, one of the famous wagon
brothers. Peter was interested in getting good outlets,
dealers, and salesmen for Studebaker products. He built
up one of the first of the big national sales organizations
that were to mean so much to American business later on.

In St. Joseph, gathering place of the new pioneers,
the ex-G.I.s of that war, and of families heading West,
Peter and a brother-in-law rented a big lot in the middle
of town and put up a wooden building 75-by-60 feet wide
to show their wagons. The rest of the lot was landscaped
as a camping and picnic ground for customers. And

customers came. Often fifty men would be camped in the lot, with their horses and mules, looking over the wagons. Sampling hard cider, playing cards, telling tall stories of Bull Run or Sitting Bull. And dreaming of the last of the free land to be reached by wheels.

THE BROTHERS' wagons were good and solid. They had what later were called accessories. A spring seat for $18. A large canvas cover for $10. Bows, mess boxes, feed boxes. You could get a wagon for $160 or one for $200.

ST. JOSEPH was only one of the selling places for Studebaker vehicles. Orders came from the Pacific coast, from Texas (open to trade again), from war-shattered towns on the Mississippi. Dealers were signed on, and in the Rockies the mountain wagon was a hit. So were wheat wagons, and log carriers with huge wheels.

As 1867 ended, the factory inventories were collected. The books showed an interesting item. "Assets $223,269.06." Bookkeeping that took care of pennies showed that their office methods were getting professional. On March 26, 1868, a new company, THE STUDEBAKER BROTHERS MANUFACTURING COMPANY, was created under the laws of Indiana. The capital was $75,000, real money, not just "assets." One third paid into the firm by each of the three partners, Clem, president; Peter, secretary; and John Mohler, the man with the eye on the money, treasurer.

Many companies — large and small — made the wagons of America, and sold them catch-as-catch-can. Convict labor built wagons for four big companies in Kansas, West Virginia, Tennessee, and Michigan. Studebaker said of one such firm, "The only man in the trade whose wagons are as good as ours is Peter Shuttler," who made wagons with convict labor at the prison at Jackson, Michigan. The canny Studebakers added, tongue in cheek, "but convicts will drive a rotten spike whenever they can."

Shuttler hired his convicts for 25 to 50 cents a day. Skilled workers at Studebaker pulled down a big $12 a week. It seemed unfair to sell for the same price as convict-made wagons, but Studebaker began to go after volume sales to bring their prices down even lower. They had now a regular payroll of 190 men, a full six-day week, seven to six, and when rush orders came in, night work. Upholsterers and painters worked under oil lamps to keep up with orders. They were busy rebuilding bigger than ever. A four-story building a block long went up under a mansard roof. A factory with 36 chimneys towered over five new sheds. A spur line connected their loading platforms with the Lake Shore and Michigan railroad.

Their finishing factory of three stories gleamed and in their photograph room pictures of their wheeled products were made. A price war soon was raging and a Studebaker wagon cost about 15 per cent under what a wagon like it would cost in New York or Chicago. They used local timber when they could, but brought in good hickory from as far away as Toledo and Cincinnati. Business held steady and grew better. New frontier markets were closer now that the Union Pacific railroad was finished, and the last rails had been laid at Promontory Point, Utah. Wagons now went by freight car.

IN 1870 the Western firm of Ames and Woodworth became the exclusive agent in San Francisco for Studebaker. Local pride was hurt and local workers feared. A California editor wrote: "Mr. Studebaker is coming once a year to find out the wants of the people. What *he* wants is *your* gold and silver . . . and he gets it." Not all native sons were such glooms. In Sacramento a company assembly plant was set up to cheering, music, and strong wine.

Running gear made in South Bend was bolted to seats, beds, and brakes made in California. Figures looked good. Thirty Studebaker wagons were shipped to California in one year. Six hundred came in the next year, among them a big quartz wagon for a state still shaking gold from the earth.

But the big customer was as always the man with the hoe and bull-tongued plow. Studebaker's sales motto was: "Our house is founded on the farmer." Peter, and Studebaker salesmen, were fixtures at state fairs, farm shows, and Grange meetings. They collected many trophies and blue ribbons as the best makers of farm equipment.

The South was slowly, painfully, coming back to life, shaking off carpetbaggers and hooded riders and memories of the late war. Studebaker opened a shop in Atlanta and produced a one-horse wagon with short couples for the Georgia market trade.

They sent out booklets, handbills, posters, and took ads in the local newspapers. So did their rival wagonmakers: Shuttler, Kansas, Milburn, and Whitewater wagons. Whitewater attacked them in an ad:

> NINE REASONS — are given why the "Studebaker" is the best wagon. The judges at the recent St. Louis fair must have thought there were at least ten the other way, for they gave the *"Whitewater"* wagon two first premiums, one on the brake and one on the wagon.

The brothers retaliated:

> THE TENTH — reason why the Whitewater wagon received even a passing notice at the St. Louis Fair: BECAUSE the justly celebrated and fully warranted STUDEBAKER FARM WAGON with SLOPE SHOULDER SPOKE is never placed in competition with wagons that every intelligent Christian mechanic KNOWS to be so much their inferior. FARMERS DON'T BE DECEIVED but get a wagon that everybody knows is the BEST.

God was on the side of the Slope Shoulder Spoke, it seemed.

Studebaker knew how to keep in the public eye. In 1871 they gave away a wagon to the farm school of the State University of Columbia, Missouri. They were always willing to have public weight-carrying contests with rival wagon firms. They once won such a contest by moving 21,024 pounds of wheat 20 feet. The wagon held up. It didn't do the horses any good, Peter said.

It wasn't all just making and selling. There were good times and bad. General Custer made his last stand on the Little Big Horn, separated from his supply train of Studebakers under General Reno. Studebaker supplied most of the army wagons for the Western army posts. Custer's death became a legend (and a beer poster), but there was a feeling that if he had stayed with his wagon train and not divided his command he would have died with his boots off in bed.

Panic came and went. Mrs. O'Leary's cow kicked over the lamp that burned down Chicago. Jay Cooke's banking house closed; Washington and Wall Street scandals didn't help business.

Fire was also a problem at Studebaker. With lots of wood, vats of paint, spread-out lumber piles, and drying yards there always was the danger of burning to the ground. The first big fire hit on a June evening in 1872. Two floors of expensive machinery and their whole stock of finished woodwork were a total loss of $70,000. Carrying only $20,000 insurance, they proudly said, "Work will be resumed in all departments in 60 days, maybe in 30." They had saved enough wood for ten thousand wagons and they went to work on the City of South Bend to put in proper water lines.

THE PANIC OF 1873 came along. Banks, manufacturers, railroads, and retailers all took it on the chin. The Studebakers managed to turn the panic prices to their advantage.

Pig iron went from $57 a ton to $16. Freight rates fell
So they built cheaper and better wagons and hunted markets. It was one of the virtues of the American system — as
the brothers saw it — to put one over on their rivals by
passing on a good buy to their customers. And often some
rival firm did the same thing to them. It was the system
of free enterprise that J.M. approved of all his life. Its
practical results were cheaper and better wagons.

First vehicle built by Studebaker was covered wagon — the Conestoga type.

Harold S. Vance inaugurates second century of production at South Bend plant.

SOUVENIR

OF VISIT TO THE

Greatest Vehicle Works on Earth

BEING THE PLANT OF

Studebaker Bros. Mfg. Co.

LOCATED AT

SOUTH BEND, IND.

J. M. STUDEBAKER, President
GEORGE M. STUDEBAKER, Vice-President

CLEMENT STUDEBAKER, Treasurer
J. M. STUDEBAKER, Jr., Secretary

Frontispiece of booklet published 50 years ago for firm's golden anniversary

The Studebaker Brothers

Founders of the Present Corporation of Studebaker Bros. Mfg

Henry Studebaker born in East Berlin, Adams Co., Pa., 5th, 1826; died May 2d, 1895.

Clement Studebaker, President was born March 12th, 1831, at Gettysburg, Adams Co., Pa., and died Nov. 1901.

Peter E. Studebaker, Treasurer, was born in Ashland Co., O., April 1st, 1836; died Oct. 12th, 1897.

Jacob F. Studebaker, Secretary, was born in Ashland Co., O., May 26th, 1844; died Dec. 17th, 1887.

John Mohler Studebaker, Vice-President, was born in Adams Co., Pa., Oct. 10th, 1833, is the only surviving son of John Studebaker.

Of the founding brothers only John M. witnessed the company's 50th birthday.

LABOR OMNIA VINCIT

Some Interesting Facts and Figures About the Studebaker Factories

Manufacturing departments and lumber yards occupy
101 acres.

Number of stationary engines in daily use, 11.

Capacity of horse-power, 2500.

Horse-power of boilers, 2050.

Number of arc lamps used in factory, 235.

Number of steam pumps, 8.

Number of iron-working machines, 312.

Miscellaneous machines, 87.

Number of feet of line shafting, 6800.

Number of pulleys on line shaft, 2000.

Number of feet of lumber used annually, about
8,000,000.

Total floor surface of all factories, 40 acres.

Horse-power in daily use, 1550.

Number of boilers in daily use, 9.

Number of dynamos in daily use, 13.

Number of incandescent lamps used in factory, 1250

Number of wood-working machines, 683.

Number of elevators, 12.

Total number of machines, 1082.

Number of feet of belting, 49,000.

Aggregate length of all the belting, over 7 miles.

Number of feet of lumber on hand, approximately
55,000,000.

Employes in machine shop to keep machines in proper
order, 72 men.

A page of souvenir booklet pointed up Studebaker's half-century of growth.

By 1902 company also had sales representation in every part of the world.

In wide use during Civil War, Studebaker wagons are seen on James River in landing supplies for Grant's army for coming Battle of the Wilderness.

World War II Studebaker trucks being road-tested at company's 800-acre pro ground. Wartime output also included tracked vehicles and bomber engines

Vorkmen boring rims for spoke tenons in wheel division of early wagon works.

mpleted auto bodies are lowered two at a time from a floor above through an opening onto their chassis assemblies moving along final assembly lines.

First blacksmith shop is shown at left. Other buildings were added in 1857.

Within 25 years, South Bend was the site of world's largest wagon works.

Present South Bend plant contains 126 acres of manufacturing floor space. Other plants are in Los Angeles, New Brunswick, N. J., and Hamilton, Canada.

Kurowski and son James are among 2,000 father-son teams in company employ.

1904 Studebaker.

1919 Big Six.

1939 Champion.

1947 Champion.

H. S. Vance, Chairman of the Board and President.

PROGRESS AND POLITICS

In 1872 the firm hired 325 men and built 6,950 vehicles. By 1874 they employed 500 men and were turning out 11,050 vehicles. And business done was up from $688,000 to a cool one million in 1875.

A second fire — a big one — came in 1874 and this time two thirds of their entire works were in ruins. They rebuilt, their advertisements told how, and they now were "The Largest Vehicle House in the World!" They rebuilt of good solid brick and covered 20 acres. Five railroads came right into their yards. And now new pulleys, cranes, power hammers, vats, and belts did their part in making wagons faster. A 200-horsepower Brown cutoff engine gave plenty of power. And their line of wagons now ran from a Nevada-type mine wagon that weighed two tons, to a two-wheeled cart.

NEW FAMILY blood was added to the firm. Young Jacob, who had a red beard, took charge of the carriage factory, making sulkies and even five-glass landaus. All the brothers were bearded. And were no longer the farm boys, the schoolteachers, the general store clerks, or mining town types of their youth. They had filled out in girth and beard, and wore well-cut clothes and the proper number of watch chains. They looked what they were: solid merchant princes. When the nation was 100 years old, and preparing a great fair in Philadelphia for its centennial, Mr. P. O'Brien, foreman of the Studebaker painting department, executed a full-length oil painting of the five brothers. It was a rich bit of work, solid and full of a homey realism; not the fancy brushwork of John Singer Sargent, painting Newport society, or Charles Dana Gibson, lining the oil and wheat and beef millionaires and their beautiful daughters in New York. The brothers liked it fine. It was a "spitting likeness." And they would exhibit at the Philadelphia World's Fair. In art as in wagons, they knew what they liked. Solid and not too damn fancy.

EVERYBODY was going to the fair that year, the biggest world's fair ever, its avenues and buildings at Fairmount Park, just outside Philadelphia, full of the wonders of a great nation finding itself in its first hundred years. Peter Studebaker, sales manager, came to Philadelphia with two exhibits. A wagon made all of rare bird's-eye maple, with a running gear of golden oak and everything polished like gold. Seat springs nickel-plated and all iron parts of imported Swedish iron, hand-forged. Inlaid letters read: CENTENNIAL S. B. MFG. CO. Modest enough, and the job costing $700. There was also a carriage lined with a brown satin chagrin at $14 a yard. The entire carriage was enclosed in a French plate glass box joined by black walnut trim. There were American flags at the corners and a clockwork sign spinning out the words:

LARGEST WAGON AND CARRIAGE BUILDERS
IN THE WORLD.

The nation was 100 years old. The founding fathers, everyone said, wouldn't have known the place. It was full of inventors, new tools, and a desire to keep going hell-for-leather. The Studebakers, the rail-layers, the road-makers, the telegraph poles — all spelled out the full century of a new, growing country.

"Lucky" Baldwin of San Francisco, millionaire and gambler, liked the Studebaker specials and bought them both after the fair closed.

The next year Studebaker had its own party. It celebrated its silver jubilee on Founder's Day, February 16. Two hundred of the best people, the family, the firm, and the top citizens of South Bend sat down to dinner. Imported fancy grub and the South Bend Cornet Band performed. Three boxes of good cigars were done away with. Clem, as president, made a speech. He said in part:

> The interest of the employer and the employee are identical. Capital cannot succeed without labor; nor can labor expect its reward without capital. What is to the interest of one is to the interest of the other.

This was pretty advanced thinking for those days. Some people felt the Studebakers were wild-eyed radicals . . .

Clem had been clear to Europe and had opened up European markets for the firm. He was getting a wider outlook on life. In 1877, sales reached $1,107,000. Next year the brothers showed their wagons in Paris, Clem being appointed "United States Commissioner to the Paris Exposition," an honor, John Mohler said, that didn't even pay for his cigars. Clem presented a Studebaker army wagon to the French War Department where it was housed in the artillery museum. The fair gave them a silver medal for the wagon.

Back in the U.S.A., President Hayes drove around the grounds of a Minneapolis fair in a five-glass Studebaker landau as did a rival, James G. Blaine. It was smart to own one, the best people felt. The Catholic clergy of the diocese of Chicago presented their bishop with a fancy job: a Studebaker berlin glass-fronted coach, lined with imported red Morocco leather and weighing half a ton. The rig, with horses, lap robes, and harness, cost $3,000. A high price in those days of the full value for the dollar. Steaks were 20 cents a pound, and eggs 12 cents a dozen. Bread was four cents a big loaf, and rent for a good house was $12 a month.

In November, 1877, General Grant returned from his famous trip around the world and in Chicago got a Welcome Home parade. The press shouted, "The greatest living general who has just concluded the grandest trip around the world, entered with his old comrades at the head of the longest procession ever witnessed in the great city of Chicago in the world's standard carriage, the celebrated Studebaker landau, drawn by six horses and driven by the manager of the extensive livery department of the Palmer House of Chicago.

This was the same Sam Grant who had driven an old Studebaker farm wagon, and once worried about where his next drink was coming from.

It was time, the brothers thought, to enjoy their success a bit. Clem became the first vice-president of the Carriage Manufacturers' Association. Peter went into politics, a power behind the Republican party machine. J.M. traveled abroad with his family and bowed his American knee when he and his wife were presented to Queen Victoria. He also bought a big farm and built a big house on it and stocked it with Jersey cows, his favorite kind. There was a deer park, and 30,000 dollars' worth of furniture from New York City. The library had an ebony ceiling and there was room for it to "contain sufficient high-toned literature." No list of books kept there has come down to us. But

John Mohler wasn't much of a reader anyway. "History," he once said, "is anything that can happen."

The need for wheels kept up. The world was growing smaller, but oddly enough the more progress it made in cutting time and space the more transport it needed. The refrigerator car had been invented and 7 million dollars' worth of beef had been shipped frozen to England. Frozen meat meant bigger farms, more feed; that meant more farming; more farming meant more wagons. A new milling process increased by three fifths the yield from ground grain by using chilled steel rollers, and the world ate more American wheat than ever before.

Farmers began to spend money on things like fancy carriages and five-glass Studebaker landaus. They no longer cleaned out the manure wagon for a trip to town. It was better in a Studebaker sulky behind two fast-stepping, matched bays. For the city, the best people bought broughams, clarences, phaetons, runabouts, victorias, and tandems; names that meant as much in their day as sedans, roadsters, and station wagons mean to us.

Studebaker made a few four-in-hands. Coaches smart enough to carry a dozen of the best people in style and top hats. They had red wheels, gold-plated lamps, yellow trim, and the smart driver cracked a 15-foot braided whip over the fashionably cropped tails of a matched team of four or even six horses. It wasn't cheap. It cost over $20,000 to buy a full outfit and run it for a year. So Studebaker did most of its business in farm wagons. The frontier was fenced in. The deer and wild turkey were going to join the dead mountain men. The farm, cultivated and usually mortgaged, moved on well-kept wheels.

It was getting easier to drive out into the country and to come to town. Some smart man had found out about the pitch beds on the island of Trinidad and what a fine road surface they made. Streets were being paved, low spots drained, and surfacing cleaned up a lot of roads as business grew. Tar, gravel, and wooden blocks began to replace a lot of the rough cobblestones.

THE RAWHIDE and axed-timber civilization was being replaced by steel. A lot of people went in for the new-fangled low bicycle, and there was talk of it replacing the horse. But that was nonsense, and while the brothers thought once about making a bicycle in their plants, they decided in the end they could concentrate only on horse-drawn vehicles. The brothers didn't rush into every new fad or fashion. They kept on expanding the use of their wagons. They made waste-disposal trucks, street cleaning, and sweeping apparatus and even fire engines.

In the end of the first quarter of 1880, Clem wrote something on a bit of paper and passed it to John Mohler. "That's my estimate of the gross sales for this year."

J.M. read the figures: $1,500,000. He said, "Only a fool would lay bets against that."

THAT YEAR the presidential campaign was going hot and heavy, Garfield against General Hancock. Clem and Peter were strong Republicans. The major issue was tariff. How to keep out cheaply made products from abroad so the American worker and American owner could continue his high pay and high income. The brothers' wagons as they saw it were "mostly iron and labor" . . . and cheap iron and cheap labor from abroad could lower wages and in-come. Peter decided to make some speeches and explain this to the workers. Speaking at the Workingmen's Club of South Bend, he said:

> It is a favorite theme of some of the Democrats to abuse Republican manufacturers. Do they remind you that the American laborer can buy more flour, more meat and potatoes with his wages than any other laborer can in any

other country on the face of the globe? Do they remind you that while a small profit on a large business will make your employer rich, at the same time a small loss on the same business will break him up? No! They tell you none of these things, but they try to impress upon you that your employers are tyrants and robbers!

Workmen, I know what it is to be poor. I know what it is to work for fifty cents a day and board myself. I know what it is to run barefoot. I know what it is to wish for the first pair of boots. I know what it is to wish for the first white shirt. I know what it is to live week in and week out on mush and milk. I know what it is to live for weeks without butter. I know what it is to sleep three in a bed and one in the middle. I know what it is to stand on the outside of a circus tent, and hear the music and the clown within and wish I had a quarter to take me in. I know more, I know what it is to look wishfully in a showcase filled with gingerbread and wish I had a penny to buy some. Knowing these things from hard experience, I say it makes my blood boil to hear any man say one word that will tend to encourage a man in a waste of time and idleness.

The brothers belonged to a more rigid time. The name Studebaker had become famous in an era of moving frontier migrations. They had helped save the Union—and they changed with the times—but as the above speech shows—they remained close to the ideas and ideals of their upbringing. It was a national pattern and so as the nation changed there were to be many conflicts—that the nation came through it into the American Century in a declining European world—shows how solid certain our bedrock ideas are—or were.

A LETTER FROM ZANZIBAR

Peter's speeches may have made a lot of converts among the workers, but at first he couldn't make a dent in John Mohler. J.M. didn't at all see why every businessman had to be a Republican. Rival firms began to spread rumors that every worker at Studebaker was forced to vote as Peter demanded. Peter offered $1,000 to anyone who could offer proof of such pressure. John Mohler frowned and decided maybe he too had been converted. His reason for entering the true faith appeared in concrete form on the Monday before the election. He wrote a letter to the press:

> I have been a supporter of the Democratic party all my life and have always voted the ticket. I have never taken an active part in politics, always believing every American citizen should use his own judgment and follow the dictates of his own conscience in casting his vote. After an honest and careful observation and consideration for the future welfare and prosperity of this country; in the interests of the black man as well as the white; the poor man as well as the rich; I believe it to be the duty of every loyal citizen, north and south, to support the Republican party of today. So I shall, if I live, cast my first Republican vote for Garfield and Arthur tomorrow."

In the South they tried to start a boycott of Studebaker wagons. But the election came, passed, and things went on as usual. At the next presidential election, Mr. Blaine —a high-tariff man—visited the South Bend plant which was decorated with signs: "Protection protects the laborer and the laborer protects the world." "The fruits of the protective tariff—our comfortable homes." A far cry from the Eastern industrialists who had said, "God has placed the rich on earth to take care of the poor."

The Democrats foamed and shouted, and the citizens of Dodd, Texas, sent a hot letter to the Studebakers:

> Gentlemen: Since the information that you threatened to disenfranchise your workers who have failed to vote as you directed, we have this day made arrangements to purchase one of your wagons, "coal oil" same and burn it in the presence of the voters of this precinct. The event will be duly advertised and published, with a request that the press of the state copy. We burn the Studebaker wagon without knowing who will be President. We burn it in the same spirit that the tea was thrown overboard in Boston harbor in 1776.

A wagon was burned. There is no information as to whether it was also tarred and feathered. Wagon-burning became a new Southern sport. Nine hundred Studebaker workers, most of them Democrats, signed a statement that they were not pressured and intended to vote Democratic if they felt like it. John Mohler said that "only ijets" would burn a wagon, and anyway the wagons used as Southern fuel, had been, he had found out, worn-out stuff. He also quoted, in private, General Sherman's statement, "If I owned Hell and Texas, I'd rent out Texas and live in Hell."

ELECTIONS or not, progress went on at South Bend. In November, 1880, electric lights were turned on at the plants; they were carbon arc lamps installed at the cost of $3,800. The Polish and Hungarian workers who crowded the plants cheered. They turned out the wagons faster under the new lights. A new wagon every six minutes. Sales were over $1½ million. One hundred thousand miles of railroad line now moved Studebaker wagons to customers by fast freight.

The wagons had a good history behind them. Some of the original stock was still in use on the salt plains of Utah. Hundreds were going to North Africa and to the veld country of the Boers.

1884 BROUGHT a new panic. Someone once figured out that the fast-growing country had a real big panic every seven years. Sales dropped suddenly by $152,000. The next year came a big fire. The main Studebaker works were not destroyed, but $85,000 of seasoned lumber went up in smoke.

To offset this loss, in Chicago Jacob opened a fancy salesroom and carriage plant. Set between the Auditorium and the Art Institute, it was quite a place. Jacob, the youngest brother, finished this job and died. The first death among the brothers.

HARD times don't last forever, at least they didn't then. By 1887 things were humming again. Sales reached $2 million at South Bend. The brothers studied a few figures. Since 1868, the year of their charter, they had collected in sales $22,197,000. Dividends were, however, as rare as hens' teeth, almost. The brothers didn't like paying them. They had paid out less than a million and a half since 1868. But in 1887 they took their thumbs off the safety valve and paid out $200,000.

With dividends and business good, the brothers spread themselves a bit. Peter dived into the Chicago real estate market in a big way. Clem decided to become a country squire and toss together a castle for himself of Indiana cobblestone (the most depressing of building materials, but solid). Set in fine lawns and gardens, it was the biggest and most costly pile ever put up in the state. It was called Tippecanoe Place, in honor of "good friend Harrison," who had ridden into the White House on the slogan. The housewarming came a little early. The huge castle burned to the ground two days before it was ready to open. The cellar ballroom remained unharmed, however, and here, among the blackened rafters, Clem gave a party for 100 guests. Six months later the place was rebuilt, good as new.

J.M. gave a fancy wedding feast, one of the biggest of the year, for one of his children. . . . And so the Studebaker brothers were accepted as real genuine American Millionaires of the Gilded Age.

WHEN Harrison became president, in 1889, he ordered a set of Studebaker carriages and harnesses for the White House. The bill was itemized as:

Landau.	.$1,600
Brougham	1,300
Victoria	1,500
Mail Phaeton	850
Mail Buggy	450
Set of double harness for landau	550
Set of double harness for brougham . . .	350
Set of single harness	225
Robes, whips, coachmen's livery	300
TOTAL	.$7,075

Today, one stock model, of a top-priced car, with a few extras like bullet-proof glass, and steps for the Secret Service men, costs more.

STUDEBAKER had done other service to the state of Indiana and South Bend. About 100 businesses and factories came to join them. Plows, sewing machines, farm tools, toys, part makers, and lumber products began to be part of South Bend. Studebaker set up outposts. In Portland, Oregon, the spruce forests supplied the stuff for wagon bodies (at half the cost of South Bend timber). And the big plant was still being enlarged, improved, and rebuilt on the home grounds. It now covered nearly 100 acres. Twenty big boilers, 16 dynamos, 16 bolted-to-floor engines, 1,000 pulleys, 600 wood and iron working machines, seven miles of belting, steam pumps by the dozens, and 500 arc and incandescent lamps making white light over all.

They were no longer just simple wagon-makers of a few popular-priced types. A lot of gilding and silvering was popular. Red leathers, fancy varnishes, were being used in the stock models on their huge lists.

Can you identify these?

Canopy-top surrey	Four-in-hand coach
Brougham	Victoria
Curtain rockaway	Landau
Coupe rockaway	Spider phaeton
Tandem cart	Runabout
Fancy-parcel wagon	Goddard buggy
Extension-front brougham	Hunting trap

Or try these on your memory:

Road wagon	Three-seat mountain wagon
Queen phaeton	Extension-top phaeton
Cabriolet	Mail buggy
Wagonette	Four-in-hand break

Studebaker was part of the Economic Revolution that was to take the country so far as a world power in the few decades from the Civil War to the twentieth century. Like the McCormick reaper, the Howe and Singer sewing machines, they helped make a frontier and seacoasts into a comfortable civilization. The little shop was passing. In 1868 "Joe" Hinds, who had once long ago hired John Mohler to make wheelbarrows in Hangtown, gave up and came to South Bend to hunt for work. The big factory had won over the small-shop craftsman.

John Mohler grinned and made Hinds assistant foreman in the wagon works. He worked his way up in time to plant superintendent . . . a job he held until his death in 1879. The gay days in the West were only the stuff of popular novels soon.

With the passing of the lone craftsman, companies had the big money and fancy processes to get at the iron ore around Lake Superior, to exploit the coke and coal and oil of·Pennsylvania, to go deeper into the silver lodes of Nevada, to land-dredge for gold in California in new ways.

The Studebakers had begun as skilled private craftsmen — but by their very success in using their skill to bring cost down and quality up, they helped change the face of the nation and made slow hand-skills old-fashioned.

And the world was turning its attention to America, marveling at its methods and its engineering. Orders came to South Bend from Russia, India, Brazil, Norway, Spain, Egypt. And at last, Zanzibar. John Mohler was forty-seven when this letter came to the brothers:

Zanzibar, 20 July, 1880

Messrs. Studebaker Bros.,
    South Bend, Ind.

Gentlemen, — I hereby beg to address you these few lines, and am glad to say that I have seen your illustrated catalogue of carriages, sent by one of my friends from

England, from which I chose two for His Highness, the Sultan of Zanzibar, and, wrote to my agents, the Messrs Maciean, Marris & Co., of London, asking them to order from you at once; but I did not receive from them any information about this till this date.

I therefore request you kindly to inform me whether my said agents ever ordered from you such carriages. Please send me a reply, as His Highness is anxious to have the carriages at once.

My address is as follows:

> Peera Dewjee
> In h.g., the Sultan's Service
> Zanzibar, Africa

How it would have amused their father Old John. But Old John had died at the good ripe age of seventy-nine in December of 1877. It was only after the death of his father that J. M. and his wife Mary, had stopped being Dunkards. They now attended the Presbyterian Church of South Bend. And when J.M. turned Republican, the South Bend *Tribune* wrote, "Indiana has in the Studebakers just as good timber for *cabinet* material as it has for *wagons*."

But John Mohler said no thanks. He wasn't interested in politics, only wheels. And the seasoned timber that went into them.

"LABOR OMNIA VINCIT!"

The Studebakers were always able to live at ease and at peace with people. Their labor relations were always good. They faced their problems honestly and solved them. As the country grew, the demand for manpower grew, and the birth rate of the native-born wasn't enough to keep the wheels rolling. Immigrants were invited in in floods. In 1882, nearly a million came into the country. South Bend drew many of them. Poles, Magyars, and Czechs. They made good wagon men, knew how to use tools and their hands, and enjoyed hard work. Letts, Jews, Lithuanians, Greeks, Slovaks, Croats, and many others came. From slums, ghettos, bleak farms, dark forests, chilly seaports, they came to earn a birthright and a living wage. South Bend trained them, paid them, and took care of their welfare. Fifty per cent were Poles or Hungarians. Their grandsons became, in many cases, "The Fighting Irish" of Notre Dame's best football teams at South Bend.

The Studebakers' interest in their workers wasn't the old-fashioned one of taking soup to the sick or tipping people silver dollars. John Mohler wrote privately to his brother Peter:

> As capital tightens and concentrates its grip on a
> society by an inevitable condensation into huge corporate

> powers, so labor strives and struggles to better its conditions by organization and assertion of its rights. This is a truism of which we are only seeing the beginning.

There was a realism about that, and healthiness, that paid off in a labor relationship so good it was the envy of many a giant corporation in America.

With the times Studebaker changed its motto from: "Owe No Man Anything But to Love One Another," that Old John had put over his Gettysburg forge, to "Always Give a Little More Than You Promise." Now the brothers wanted something with the dignity of Latin. Finally it was decided on: *Labor Omnia Vincit!*

John Mohler had several interpretations of it. "Labor Conquers All," or "Work Always Wins." Labels meant a lot in the wagon trade. The most popular buggy they ever made was called the Izzer Buggy. It got its name in an odd way. Peter overheard a horse trader extolling his animals to a farmer. One had won a hauling contest, another a blue ribbon at a county fair, and so on. All some years past. The farmer snorted: "They're all has-beens. I don't want a *wuzzer*. What I want is a *izzer*."

So the new buggy became the Izzer. Radio comics had not yet sharpened the ears of America to the sound of good solid corn, but we are still a nation who prefers an *izzer* to a *wuzzer* in anything we buy.

STUDEBAKER was getting able to ride the run-of-the-mill panics that came from time to time. But 1893 wasn't just a panic. It was a PANIC! Banks, railroads, industry, were caught in one of those storms of overexpansion, stock speculation, silver and gold manipulation, that ended in armies of unemployed and a sudden drop in buying power. Bread came before wagons, shoes before reaping machines.

At South Bend men were turned away, the chimney smoke wasn't as black as usual.

John Mohler went to New York and down to Wall Street. He wrote a lot of paper reading, "I promise to pay. J.M. Studebaker." It was always acceptable: a fine old-fashioned script of big sums.

For a while the plants closed down. The workers wondered why suddenly now there was no demand for their solid-made wagons. Peter tried to explain it, but it was a little over their heads. Why a depression? Peter answered:

> It has been precipitated by a lack of confidence. The whole world doubts in the ability of our government to maintain its silver certificates at a parity with gold, and fears we might eventually do business on a silver basis.

The Poles and Hungarians shook their heads. That didn't help much in getting bread or in clothing big broods. It didn't make it easier to sit around and not use the big muscles skilled in making wheels.

AFTER five weeks a limited number of men were called back to make wagons. Wages were cut. The press said as much as 35 per cent. J.M. said no, not that much, but if they wanted figures, sales had fallen $400,000. And dividends had been passed for the first time since 1876.

There was talk of strikes and there were small strikes, but Studebaker weathered the storm. They didn't mind organization if the workers wanted it. The workers themselves protested when rumors about the plants got about. They said in print:

> We wish to say in the most emphatic manner, that we are not partial to strikes of any kind. We do not look upon our employer as a "robber and oppressor." We believe

that our employer must do a profitable business in order to pay us a reasonable rate of wages, and we are ready and willing at all times to assist in making his business profitable.

NOT ALL of American industry relationships were good as those at Studebaker. It was a time of the horrors of the railroad strikes with troops being used against workers. Of bombings and murders in the mine fields. Of hungry armies of men, ready for anything, marching on Washington. Of oil interests using machine guns and barb wire, of the railroading of working men to prison, of the terror of the private police importing hoodlums and thugs to protect property. At Studebaker there was John Mohler talking a much different tune. No private police, thugs, or barb wire.

> I feel that you deserve the same right to be proud of the growth and prosperity of our institution that we have ourselves. I consider that every employee, so long as he is an employee, is a stockholder of the concern. So long as he gets his compensation he gets his daily bread out of it, and that is all I get. God has enabled me, without being your superior, to reach a little higher power; to afford a little more luxury in living, but that is all. Happiness and contentment make the true wealth of this world.

TWO DREADFUL years followed. Years the locusts ate, when hunger and dust walked the factory runs, two years that made all men grim, and the faces of little children were pale, their eyes staring into space. Then, as suddenly as it had begun, this depression faded. By the last months of 1895 Studebaker was working a 12-hour shift to fill its influx of new orders. There would be full plowing in the spring, and markets for the fruit of the fields. There would be bread and meat on the tables of the workers. And all too soon, as J.M. knew, all would forget how hard it had been. It was a new country and it had no time to face any way but forward.

There was a new song about the problems of the farmer . . . and a real hint of how to cure them:

> The rain and shine and dew came down
> The farmers' crops would fill the town.
> But worn-out wagons spoil it all.
> When prices suit, he cannot haul.
>
> Oh, farmers all! Poor farmers all!
> To save your cash on you I call.
> For Studebaker offers you
> The very best that he can do.
> Then to it quick your horses hitch.
> 'Twill last until you all get rich.

There was no glancing back. Times were again good. The signs at buyers' parties at the South Bend plants read: EXCURSION TO THE LARGEST VEHICLE FACTORY IN THE WORLD! ANNUAL CAPACITY 75,000 VEHICLES!

There was 50 million feet of lumber always in the yards, hundreds of shapes of steel, 300 tons of them, and the wagons in storage for buyers ran from 12 to 15 thousand. The plating rooms plated in nickel, in silver, and even in gold. Assembly crews turned out sections, made the axles, hubs, seats, boxes, wheels spin.

AND THERE were women now in the plants. Yes, the Studebaker brothers didn't see anything wrong in a woman earning her living. A woman clerk was hired at the end of the 1880's for the collection department. Her training for the job was rather odd. A report reads: "She was a very good Methodist, and didn't encourage levity." A year later Miss Ford appeared at a typewriter, the first woman stenographer in South Bend. Miss Ford was a Gibson Girl type, and her typewriter was the size of a small iron stove. But it saved time and made fast copies that looked neat.

There was a lot of work for typewriters now. South Africa, Australia, China, South America, were asking for wagons. In many parts of the world *Studebaker* meant *Wagon*.

A south sea island, Honolulu, bought street sprinkler carts, African explorers on safaris didn't depend on just native heads to carry all their gear; a special wagon helped. In 1898 the Spanish-American War was about due. Frederic Remington, the artist, sketching in Cuba for his publisher, had wired home he saw no war. Hearst had wired back, "You provide the pictures, I'll provide the war." It came and the army quartermaster asked Studebaker for five hundred wagons stenciled U.S.A. "within 36 hours." Twenty-four hours later, stencils still damp, they were on their way. The army asked South Bend to be ready to ship wagons indefinitely.

THE HORSELESS CARRIAGE

Our twentieth century broke out in a rash of troublesome wars, and Studebaker wagons saw action in the Boxer Rebellion in China. Studebaker wagons crossed the war-torn veld in South Africa. Most of the wagons used against the Boers, at one time, were from South Bend. General Lord Roberts made their ability part of the British War Record:

> They proved superior to any other make of either Cape or English manufacture. The superiority of these vehicles was doubtless due to the fact that in America such wagons are largely used for the carriage of goods as well as for military transport. It may be added that they cost considerably less than Bristol pattern wagons.

An earnest, bull-dog faced young reporter on the field of battle was named Winston Churchill. He was fitted up with a newspaper office and sleeping space in a Studebaker wagon. Both he and the wagon were captured by the Boers. Churchill escaped, but the Boers were too canny to let the wagon get out of their hands again.

IT CERTAINLY looked as if the future belonged to the wagon forever. But the *Carriage Journal*, the Bible of the horse-and-wagon builders, carried one odd story that the brothers read:

> A man in Massachusetts has made a steam carriage which will run under its own power. It weighs only 400 pounds and can carry two persons at once. It has the appearance of an ordinary carriage in front, except there are no provisions made for a horse. The wheels are of cycle make and four in number. The boiler and engine are just in the rear of the seat and give the carriage the appearance of a fire engine. The steering part consists of a crank wheel on the footboard, so that the engineer can steer and attend to the engine at the same time.

It was a cloud "no bigger than a man's hand." But John Mohler did go to Benton Harbor to look over a gasoline engine. They tinkered with some experimental horseless carriages on their own. Meanwhile, the demand for wagons went on. The horse on iron toes was still the power behind, or rather, before the wheels.

GET-UP-AND-GO had always been the American motto, and now there was coming to makers of transportation a machine, a thing of iron, shaped and cunningly made, to use the power of lightning and fire to carry man faster and farther than anyone had yet moved him over the face of the earth. In America along the roads they were to wake up and wonder. The cruel mountaintops from which the wagon folk had looked across at the promised land would echo soon with the bang of a motor geared to wheels. Where J.M. and the gold hunters, the buffalo and the Indian runner, where the Pony Express riders and the war parties had passed, here would come, in a generation or two, a new kind of speed and fury, mostly under control. The farm would become part of the town. The people would see each other more often. There would be reunions of faces and families.

The snorting, lurching, spine-breaking horseless carriage would become streamlined, comfortable, and purring at speeds that to the wagon trains would have been called witchcraft at the speed of sound. But the amazing thing was how quickly, in a fistful of years, the change-over would be made. But not too easy, not too smoothly. For the human element and the stubborn hardness of steel took effort and knowledge and courage to conquer. Studebaker, among others, had to put their own money and their own future into the idea that the thing would run, keep running, and not blow the world apart. Later it was easy to say, "We always knew it would work." It's always easy, later, John Mohler said, to be an armchair expert.

MORE nonsense has been written about the invention of the motor car than almost any subject, unless it's romantic love. So many men have claimed it, or its more important inventions, that it's pretty confusing to try and give the proper credits. The truth always appeared to J.M. to be the simple fact that a lot of people got excited at the same time over motor cars, and a lot of them over the same things at the same time, and overlapped.

For centuries, people had tried to make a self-moving vehicle with ideas of using wind and steam, fire and clockworks. In 1886, in Germany, one Gottlieb Daimler built a practical internal-combustion engine. Another German named Krebs decided to put such an engine, burning gasoline, in the front part of a wheeled chassis. In France and England they had the same idea. Benz, Royce, Panhard, were the Daniel Boones of the gas buggies. In America there were men like Haynes, Olds, Winton, Apperson, Stanley, Maxwell, and Duryea who liked the idea and puttered with it, and got their names on Early Stone Age motor cars. By 1895 a handful of American-made passenger cars timidly lived on our roads. By 1899 the number had mounted into the thousands.

Studebaker was moving cautiously. Clem's boy had been a colonel in the 157th Regiment of Indiana Volunteers in the Spanish-American War, and he was now excited by the idea of motor cars. So was a young man named Frederick S. Fish. In 1891 Fred Fish had become John Mohler's son-in-law. Fred was from Newark, New Jersey, a lawyer of promise, and president of the New Jersey Senate in 1887. In New York City he was a corporation lawyer and had worked for many big firms. When he married John Mohler's daughter, he entered the firm as a director and general counsel. When Peter died in 1897, he became chairman of the Executive Committee.

Fred Fish was not just a lawyer. He was an early bug on aviation, even before the Wright Brothers flew at Kitty Hawk. And he was crazy about the idea of a practical horseless carriage. In 1895 he was talking of it at Studebaker. In 1897 the firm had an engineer working on a motor vehicle. The second generation of Studebakers was enthusiastic. In November, 1900, Fred Fish was in New York City at the Madison Square Garden for the first automobile show in America. Thirty-one makers of cars, and over a dozen makers of accessories, had put the show together. The big boys in the half-empty place were Pope, Winton, Duryea, and Haynes-Apperson. Steam and electric had a small edge over gasoline as power units.

In 1901 there was an auto show in Chicago, pretty close to South Bend. That year, two deaths upset a lot of plans. In September, at Buffalo, President McKinley was shot down by an assassin's bullet. He died, and Theodore Roosevelt became president of the new nation as it turned the corner into the twentieth century. McKinley had been elected on the holy tripod of high tariff, the gold standard, and an expanding United States. No one knew what Teddy, the Rough Rider, with the big teeth and the big stick, would do to upset the applecart.

One of the worriers was Clem Studebaker, elder statesman of wagon sales, returning from London where he had been visiting with J. Pierpont Morgan and Andrew Carnegie. He stumbled and fell getting off the boat in New York. He was rushed home to Tippecanoe Place, and died there, a few weeks later, listening to the whistles of the Studebaker plants.

Henry had died on his farm, Jacob and Peter and Clem were all gone now. John Mohler was alone. He was sixty-eight. And they were talking about horseless carriages and motor cars more than ever. The firm had celebrated its golden anniversary. No other auto manufacturer was to do that until Studebaker was at the century mark. It had been a fine family of brothers. They had done a good job. They had made millions, but not in the way others had. The Astor and the Vanderbilt families had, it was said, 200 million each. Jay Gould was worth 75 million; John D. Rockefeller, Leland Stanford, Andrew Carnegie over 40 million, Marshall Field, John Wanamaker, 15 million, at least.

Now John was the last of the big Studebaker brothers . . . and the horseless wagon was what the world wanted.

In 1902 the company made electrics; as battery-powered cars were called. Five models: a trap, two runabouts, and two Stanhopes. They were small, dark, square cars, designed along the lines of carriages.

They all had the same chassis, a five-foot one-inch wheel base, stood 29 inches off the floor, weighed 1,350 pounds. Four speeds sent you hurtling along, and, on level ground only, top speed was 13 miles an hour. They had a bell, no horn, coach lamps, and carriage fenders.

Four days before the company was fifty years old they sold their first electric. It was a good season: they sold 20 electric cars that year. The catalogue said proudly:

As may be imagined, we have not been indifferent to the introduction of the horseless carriage. We have not, however, believed that it would be wise on our part or good faith toward the public to push upon the market an imperfect or immature product. We have expended a large amount of time and money in experimenting and research conducted for us by experts, in order that the machine of our adoption should be such that we could recommend and not discredit our standing in the vehicle world.

THE GASOLINE AGE

The Studebaker electrics were shown, proudly, at the Chicago Columbian exhibits. But there was no real future in such a slow car depending on batteries. Gasoline-powered cars were the talk in smart engineering circles.

Fred Fish made an exploring trip to the Garford motor plant at Elyria, Ohio. A deal was worked out for Garford to supply the chassis and motor, and Studebaker to put a body on it. In 1904 the first Studebaker-Garford was put on the market. It was big, black, and made a lot of noise. But it ran. The fad — it was "only a fad" everyone said — for horseless carriages was spreading. Everywhere people watched the new monsters on the dusty roads and shook their heads and laughed and shouted, "Git a horse." But more people bought autos. They still cost a lot and broke down sometimes. But Americans found the Studebaker-Garford fun and exciting.

In 1904 Studebaker did a business of $4,840,000, a good share of it horseless carriages. The wagon business was better than ever, too. Fred Fish was not fully pleased yet. He wanted standardized, interchangeable parts, "a car a man could almost repair himself." The Society of Automotive Engineers excited him. They had the same ideas, talked his language.

John Mohler listened and nodded and said, "We're selling more wagons than ever." They made "black marias" for the police departments, in which rode the real early Keystone cops; child carts, called "Studebaker Jrs." to be pulled by dogs or goats, and bank and mail wagons, undertaker carts of gloomy, glossy black, ice wagons, dairy and bakers' trucks, garbage wagons and *even* sleighs. In 1905 sales passed $5 million, and next year almost $7 million. The wagon was here to stay. Any "ijet" could see that.

But an odd thing happened in 1907. Sales in 1907 were $7,827,000. Most of the gains were made by the motor cars . . . *and* it was a panic year. The big Panic of 1907 — the panic, whatever else it did, didn't hurt Studebaker's automobile business. John Mohler saw some kind of lesson in this; he didn't know just what.

Get into motors deeper, the handwriting — or rather the sales figures — seemed to say . . . In 1908 there was incorporated under the laws of Michigan an Everitt-Metzger-Flanders Company. With a capital stock of a million dollars. They said they were going after the medium-priced popular-car market. Studebaker liked *that* idea and asked for the right to sell the product through their vast national sales organization as the Studebaker-E-M-F car. Studebaker bought a third of the Everett-Metzger-Flanders stock. Fred Fish insisted it was a great deal.

More than a thousand Studebaker outlets took care of the 8,132 cars turned out the first year. By 1909 the company had sold 9.5 million dollars' worth of horseless vehicles, and knew it was in the motor business for keeps. Fred Fish tried to buy up all the E-M-F stock. It had passed into the hands of J.P. Morgan and Company of Wall Street. Here Fred Fish made an offer for it, and got it. Studebaker now controlled and *owned* a motor car in its own right! They had a smooth-running group of engineers and production heads and a crackerjack sales organization. Fred and J.M. decided to cut prices to get more customers. Their "20" model, retailed at $1,000, was cut to $750.

The company was getting bigger, getting spread out in many directions. They needed to reorganize in a big way.

In 1911 it was decided to refinance and to incorporate as the Studebaker Corporation. The company discontinued the making of electric vehicles that same year. Almost 60 years after Clem and Henry opened their forge there was a new company with total assets of $57 million and a working capital of close to $14 million. But control still remained in the canny hands of the Studebaker family.

It was a test of the strength of the enterprise the Studebaker brothers had built. Now the public was offered 150,000 shares of cumulative preferred stock at 7 per cent with a par value of $100. And 300,000 shares of common stock at a par value of $100. Two New York City firms handled the financing: Goldman, Sachs & Co., and Lehman Brothers, Bankers.

Selling stock to the public was a long way, John Mohler felt, from taking off your money belt and weighing out gold nuggets brought from Hangtown. From hunting standing timber around South Bend and getting it cut and hauled to season; from buying raw iron and hammering it by hand on your own forges; from getting together your wagons and driving out in the country and selling them to the farmers for whatever you could get in trade and cash. He remembered the time they had traded a good wagon for a blind bay horse. Well, he didn't want the public to trade their good money for shoddy stuff. No matter what the young fry did with their new ideas, he would see to it that the value and the honest workmanship was still there in every wagon or auto they turned out.

It was no shock for the workers coming in on the morning shift to see the old man inspecting the wood yards to see if the timber was properly aged and dried. He never grew to love steel the way he loved wood. And once or twice a week he went down to the yards to look over the piles of timber. He didn't mind making price cuts, if the value remained. The price of their 40-horse power car was cut from $4,000 to $2,500. How the other motor companies screamed!

The "30" (naming cars like race horses and Pullman cars had not yet become fashionable) that sold at $1,250 was cut to an even $1,000. Would it hurt or help business? The end of the year showed a high of $28,500,000 in sales. That year, of all makes, America bought 160 million dollars' worth of motor cars. The wagon was taking the back roads into town. The horse looked bewildered and tired.

At South Bend everyone knew horse-and-buggy thinking was over. A new administration building was loaded to the roof with machines no one had dreamed of a few years ago. A dozen electric Gramophones for dictation, 180 telephones ("all connected," John Mohler is once said to have announced with a grin), six billing machines, two addressing machines, two checkwriters, half-a-dozen pneumatic mail tubes, a dozen clocks wired to a master chronometer. *And* 97 young girls in full bloom bent over 97 chattering typewriters. You couldn't laugh off all that progress.

John Mohler watched, and noticed they still sold a lot of wagons. He wasn't too sure about an auto in every home. And he issued a warning in his best country store prose:

> The automobile, of course, has come to stay. But when a man has no business it is a rather expensive luxury, and

I would advise no man, be he farmer or merchant, to buy one until he has a sufficient income to keep it up. A horse and buggy will afford a great deal of enjoyment, not to the great extent that an automobile will, but the buggy is not as expensive a luxury. It will pay the farmer who lives five miles from town and who has cows to milk, to buy an automobile, as he can get up at four o'clock or five in the morning, milk his cows, bring the milk to town, dispose of it and be back at his work at eight with his horses all in good shape. For this reason I say that if a person has a business, a machine is a good thing to have, but if a person has no business and no income, I should say, go slowly. An automobile is a piece of machinery and has to be looked after. It is expensive and will wear out.

John Mohler himself gave in to the auto with ease. He still, of course, kept his phaeton and his matched team of horses, but they loafed fat in the fields and weren't used a lot. Andrew Johnson, his coachman, learned to drive an automobile, more or less. They had to pay for chickens and hogs killed, and once they ran into "the south end of a cow going north." Andrew Johnson liked to get the car places on time, and, once, taking John Mohler to the bank, he misjudged his braking speed and ran part of the car into the bank itself. "The bank recovered," John Mohler said. "Its assets were in good order."

In 1910 John and Mary Studebaker had celebrated their golden wedding anniversary. Five hundred guests were there; fancy food, wine, and cigars were passed around. As John Mohler looked over his children, grandchildren, cousins, and grandcousins he marveled, "How a family keeps spreading out." There were also plant workers, and executives; many faces he didn't know. The plants were growing bigger, the organization spreading out.

FOURTEEN

REMEMBRANCE OF
THINGS PAST

The comfortable world of John Mohler was to change quickly, and it was to be a world like nothing that had gone before. It had been a good time, and a simple time for the country mostly, since the day Lee and Grant decided on a peace in the Virginia mud. And it would last, the golden weather, until, as one man said on the eve of World War I: "The lights are going out all over the world. We shall not see them relit in our times."

In those American generations between wars, there had been minor troubles and panics and depressions, but the nation had gone on growing and roaring. It was a time of apple pie picnics on the lake, and riding dusty roads in goggles and linen dusters, of drinking beer from the keg and singing slowly the old songs on the banks of the Wabash.

These times were to change, and the music was to be ragtime from the Beale Street dives, then the real Dixieland frenzy from New Orleans. The cars no longer were high and slow and full of noise, but ate dangerously into space at speeds no sane horse-and-buggy person would ever have wanted to go. The skirts were becoming tighter and higher, and the Americans were in danger of putting aside the cheroot and stogie for something called a cigarette. Boots that had walked Main Street mud were becoming high button shoes, and the derby and the peg-topped pants were disappearing with the big mustache and the last of beards on Charles Evans Hughes. When John Mohler and Mary started for California in 1912, it was just two short years before their world would be blown apart, and a new kind of pace take over the nation, a pace from which it would never recover. There would be world crises from then on, rearmament, the lost generation, bobbed hair, and the whine of gutter jazz in respectable places. They were seeing the last of their era as their train puffed its way across mountain passes toward the California coast.

THE WELCOME signs were out in California:

GLAD YOU'RE BACK
WELCOME, JOHN STUDEBAKER
IF THE CITY HAD A KEY, YOU'D GET IT
WELCOME, WHEELBARROW JOHNNY

The old folks had traveled all night, John Mohler and his wife, upriver from San Francisco, and in the morning, April 16, 1912, they were in Sacramento. Chester N. Weaver, the Studebaker manager on the coast, met them with two well-polished Studebaker touring cars. The road got worse as they got near Placerville, but the old man didn't mind. The country scene hadn't changed, but the miners' huts, the raw cuts in the earth, were gone. Placerville was forgotten a little now. Some of its old buildings were still standing. The welcome was real loud and mighty grand.

The *El Dorado Republican and Nugget* got out a special edition:

More than fifty-nine years ago a gaunt youth of 19 stepped down from an emigrant wagon and took his first look around at the country where he had come to make a fortune. In his pocket was a lone 50-cent piece. Today a kindly-faced aged man stepped down from the tonneau of a luxurious automobile and looked around him at the country where he had laid the foundation for his fortune. It was J. M. Studebaker returning to take perhaps his last look at the scenes of his early struggles.

The auto had drawn up in front of the Ohio House where on the wooden porch stood a score of grizzled men. As Studebaker stepped down from his auto he spied a face in the crowd. "Hello, Newt, you around here yet?" he said, by way of salutation.

While collecting the material for this history, the author went out to Placerville, in April, 1952, and talked to some of the citizens who still remember the visit of 1912. It was really, one old timer said, "a root, toot, and holler time." But several expressed the view that John Mohler, after a while, got a little stingy about setting up the free drinks. "He didn't like drunks."

I did find a wheelbarrow that J.M. made in his youth, and a pick ax he forged, with the letters J.M. STUDEBAKER burned by him into the old polished handle with a hot iron.

I have before me as I write, the full menu of the dinner at Placerville given for John Mohler. It is written in Western Humor, Old Style. Mark Twain, on an off day, could have composed it.

Chuck List

CHILI GULCH RIB WARMER

SLUICE BOX TAILINGS, FLAVORED WITH
CHICKEN

HIGHGRADE OLIVES   SPANISH FLAT ONIONS

CEDAR RAVINE RADISHES   COON HOLLOW PICKLES

SACRAMENTO RIVER SALMON PAVED WITH
CHEESE

INDIAN DIGGINS SPUDS

TERTIARY MOISTURE

SLAB OF COW FROM THE STATES

BANDANA FRIES WITH BUG-JUICE

LADY CANYON CHICKEN, HANGTOWN
DRESSED

WEBBERTOWN MURPHYS

SHIRT-TAIL BEND PEAS

DEAD MAN'S RAVINE ASPARAGUS

CEMENTED GRAVEL À LA EMIGRANT JANE

BUTCHER BROWN FIZZ WATER

ASSORTED NUGGETS

AMALGAM CHEESE, RIFLE CRACKERS

MAHALA'S DELIGHT EN TASSE

TEXAS HILL FRUIT

PAY DAY SMOKES   HARD PAN SMOKES

An old account of the visit ends with these words:

Max Mierson, President of the Board of Trade, on behalf of the citizens and friends, proposed the toast, "Speed the Parting Guest," bespeaking the good will and kindly wishes of the community for the man whom they are proud to refer to as their former townsman.

After singing "Auld Lang Syne," the final hand clasps were given and the company separated, many never to meet again.

FIFTEEN

THE AUTO GOES
COAST TO COAST

Back home in South Bend by the red and gold of an Indian summer, John Mohler looked around him. Progress was being made. The motor car was being perfected. There had been defects in design and manufacturing of the "20," and now something would be done about it. J.M. announced:

> Business ethics are the same regardless of product. For sixty years the Studebaker Company has backed up its goods with a guarantee showing good faith. Its relation to those who bought and used its wagons and carriages has always been considered a binding obligation. We apply this principle to our automobile business.

What this meant the whole country soon found out. Hundreds of mechanics were sent out to install improved parts, "and for nothing," in every "20" car they had sold. This ideal cost almost a million dollars in three-speed transmissions, separate exhaust manifolds, rubber insert clutches, braking surfaces, and carburetors. . . . But it paid off in good will and much newspaper space. And every Studebaker "20" in the land now ran like new.

STUDEBAKER liked public road contests against rival firms. They entered their cars in all contest runs, and almost always won. The Munsey run of 1910 had used a Studebaker-E-M-F as a pathfinder (a needed car in those days of no road maps and lost roads). The car was seen in West Point exceeding the four-mile-an-hour speed limit and ruled off the reservation. Later it frightened some horses and was fined $400 for treating nags in this cruel fashion. In every tour through rain, sand, and heat there was a Studebaker, muddy, but hood unbowed.

In 1912 there was no place else for the motor car driver to go but cross-country and a group was formed to plug for a coast-to-coast rock road, a hard-surface highway from the Atlantic to the Pacific. On October 31, 1913, celebrations were held in many states as the official dedication of the first transcontinental road, the Lincoln Highway, was opened with a roar of gasoline motors. J.M. spoke for the South Bend section of the road, by a bonfire lighting up the skies.

STUDEBAKER put out one of the first auto road maps, marking out the roads in Indiana, and telling daring drivers how to get from South Bend to Chicago, but at their *own* risk. DETOUR was often mistaken for a dirty French word.

ABROAD, in Europe, and elsewhere, the Studebaker car was a welcome import. Fred Fish opened export offices in New York City. Twenty-one million five hundred thousand dollars' worth of American cars had been sold abroad, and by 1912 Studebaker was accounting for 37 per cent of all cars exported. In the Canal Zone a fleet of Studebaker-E-M-Fs carried the mail, the cops, and the engineers. Turkey, at war with Bulgaria, bought military vehicles and artillery mounts. The roads of Europe ate dust from Studebaker cars. English dukes and Studebakers took a mutual polish.

JOHN MOHLER was eighty in 1913. The big whistles blew, the men took time off from work to celebrate. J.M. shook hands as the workers filed past; standing with seven men who had been with the firm for over 40 years. One man had been there for 48 years. J.M. was presented with a big silver loving cup. A prize had been offered by the firm for the oldest Studebaker wagon still in active daily use. Dave Clarke of Gilenton, Wisconsin, won easily. He still trucked grain and potatoes to market in a wagon bought in 1865.

It looked like a good world at peace, contented, the turmoils of the industrial revolution over. Good jobs and good wages for all. Nothing, John Mohler felt, could upset now the few years of peace ahead of him, surrounded by family, by friends, and the factory whistles blowing music in his ears.

But far away in Serbia, a few students were planning to shoot some member of the Austrian royal family. Germans were still nodding agreement as the Kaiser repeated his old phrase about their "place in the sun." In Verdun the peasants were preparing for the harvesting of their grapes. Eminent voices asserted that general wars were now impossible, because they would cost too much. There seemed no threat to continued peace.

MEANWHILE, two young men were growing up whose destiny it would be to see Studebaker through its most exciting and trying years. Two young men who were to make the company the largest independent car manufacturer in the world, and who were to create new foundries, new processes, and the designs of the modern car.

Harold Sines Vance was a boy from Port Huron, Michigan. He was alert, active, and, while his education had been simple, it had been solid. In 1910 he showed up at the Port Huron branch of E-M-F to take a job as a mechanic's apprentice. His pay amounted to 15 cents an hour. He was excited, not just by the motors but by the whole organization: its methods, its ways of doing things. But being a mechanic's helper seemed a limited kind of job. He wanted to be all over the whole shebang, be part of the whole works. He got a job in the stores division, handling parts and cataloguing, taking care of all the hundreds of little things that went into a car. From there he went into purchasing, studying, and finding out about the things that were bought, and how they were converted into parts for the cars. He learned steel, he learned sparkplugs, wires, tools, tires. He found out how to buy, how to get small parts for the plants. He met people, he traveled, he made of purchasing a full science. He became a judge of men as well as materials.

The business was young; there was a lot to learn. The Studebaker E-M-F, he saw, was made mostly in its own factory. Others bought motors, axles, tops, lights, wheels, but Studebaker made most of its components itself.

In South Bend they planned sales and models. Harold Vance moved on to E-M-F in Detroit, headquarters of the motor car business, developing his own way of doing things. Not always the way they did things in a company used to making wagons by processes just a little out of date by now. Science, the young man felt, could be used more than it had yet been used. Blacksmith methods were fine, but a car was not a wagon. It was a delicate, intricate machine, marvelous in its precision, daring in its use of the science of combustion.

THE OTHER young man of promise had been born in Chicago. He was named Paul Hoffman, and he only had one major idea: to get out of school and get into the automobile business. He was in love with autos, mad about cars. He hung around Chicago salesrooms as a boy, and he tried to talk to his family about his enthusiasms. His father nodded and didn't seem very much impressed when Paul decided the family ought to have a car. It was Paul's first big selling job.

Paul's father, at last worn down, bought a second-hand Pope-Toledo for $1,500. It wore out tires at $90 each, broke steering knuckles like teeth, at $30, and the springs went like the robins in winter, at $30 a spring. It was an open car, noisy, dusty. But Paul enjoyed the family's 60-mile trips into the then virgin country. They changed sparkplugs, repaired punctures, and pushed the car up steep grades. They got soaked in rains, boiled in summer suns, but Paul Hoffman grinned, peeled his sunburned nose, and loved motor cars.

The car left them stranded, lived in strange garages, and was rebuilt from time to time in dazzling and amazing ways. The family couldn't understand Paul's love of these big, stinking, groaning, and often repaired monsters.

In 1909 Paul was working earnestly for the dealer for Halladay cars. He was put in charge of all repairs. The staff was himself and one mechanic. Six months later he got into a car and became a salesman. If he couldn't get money he took anything in barter, and then had to trade the stuff for money to give his boss.

In 1911 he worked his way West selling a new kind of moaning auto horn. He got a job with the Studebaker dealer in Los Angeles, a Mr. Sam Smith, who liked him and taught him a few extra selling methods.

Paul Hoffman became a fabulous salesman among the yucca plants and the orange groves. Hollywood was still a country road, and water was the thing they dreamed of, lots of water to grow more oranges. He sold the early settlers and found out that the car that was simple, with accessible parts, was what the native American liked. That, and repair parts that could be bought cheap and put in with ease.

Paul sold a lot of cars. More than they had expected. One month his commissions ran to $1,000. In 1912, his heart always close to South Bend, he won an essay contest for company salesmen. One of the prizes was a trip to South Bend. He packed and went. Paul went through the plants. He made notes (even made suggestions) and at last saw John Mohler himself. . . . A dignified old man with alive, alert eyes, a big beard, sitting with dignity behind a carved desk.

I had won a national essay contest on the subject "How to Sell a Studebaker Automobile." My prize was a personal visit with J.M. Studebaker. I was escorted into Mr. Studebaker's office on the fourth floor of the administration building. He was then in his late seventies, and was seated behind an old roll-top desk slitting envelopes and putting them all into a neat pile. He said, "The boys downstairs buy scratch pads — I think it is an extravagance, a useless extravagance." That, of course, was a lesson in frugality. It was a lesson I hardly needed because my grand prize was just this visit, which itself was some evidence of frugality.

But he gave me a second, more important, reason. He said, "You're just starting out in business, and perhaps you would like to know why I think we have been successful." I assured him I would like very much to know indeed.

"It's because," he continued, "we always give our customers more than we promise. This way you hold customers, and get more customers." He waited a moment, and then added: "But don't give them too much more, or you'll go broke."

NEW BLOOD
AT SOUTH BEND

John Mohler Studebaker was eighty-one. The world was at war in 1914. It had come suddenly, after much saber-rattling and talk, after piddling little events: a pistol crack in a Serbian street and a fat man and his wife shot dead in an early motor car. An exchange of notes with a Germany using any excuse to get into a war of world conquest . . . a mobilizing of conscript armies. In Russia and England and in France, in the great diseased bulk of the Austro-Hungary collection of serf states, men armed . . . and soon the endless gray hordes of Germans were marching through neutral little countries, marching to tear the guts out of the world. The old man at South Bend was shocked . . .

These armies needed vast supplies and transportation. America had the factories, the resources, the men, and the minds to supply a world war. Industry in America felt the shock of war in a flood of orders as the belligerents cabled wildly across the Atlantic for supplies.

A NEW face and name had appeared at Studebaker backed by some tremendous and personal energy. While Harold Vance was producing in Detroit, and Paul Hoffman was selling on the coast, Albert Russel Erskine had emerged as the new strong man in South Bend. He had come into the company in 1911, as treasurer, and by 1913 had become first vice-president. He brought Harold Vance from Detroit and made him assistant treasurer.

Erskine — an early go-getter — had started his business life as a $15-a-week bookkeeper, and had gone through auditing and many financing projects with ease, having a head for figures and a strong body that drove his ideas through. It was to be the century of the big executive, Erskine felt. He had not grown up with Studebaker, and when he came to it he saw it as a sprawling industrial empire that needed tighter organizing. He organized it, and the war orders that he filled made it greater than ever. England at war needed wagons, 3,000 of them at once. A cable asked for 20,000 sets of harnesses, 60,000 sets of saddles and blankets. The horse was not yet dead in 1914, and the British mounted guardsmen were the handsomest men in Europe. The company hired new men, new space, and turned out its first thousand sets of harness.

Fred Fish, now president of the company, went to Europe. In London he negotiated with the British War Office direct. England was popular in this country, and the Morgan loans were not yet called the only reason for our support of the true fighters for our civilization. The Hun was butchering in Europe with German skill, and in New Jersey a Studebaker plant was bombed and burned out. A week later it was back in business. The orders for saddles fell off as trench warfare took over.

Studebaker made artillery wheels, drinking water carts, ambulances, and all the trappings of war. The British War Office gave South Bend an order for 5,000 military caterpillar trucks. The endless wheeled caterpillar treads were the first platforms for the first tanks. The English expanded the idea of caterpillar treads into an armored tank in 1916. They threw a handful of tanks into trench warfare, broke through the Germans, panicked them by surprise. But they were not ready to follow through their success. War Office thinking was moss-covered, so the British tossed away a chance to win the war quickly. By the time the British had come around to believing in tanks, the Germans had their own ironclad monsters ready. The French and Russians sent buying missions to South Bend. War orders came in faster than they could be filled.

IN 1915 Studebaker, expanding and busy, reorganized its top brass. J.M. stepped up at the age of nearly eighty-two to honorary president, Erskine became president. Fred Fish became chairman of the board. It was time for doing and making. Erskine was a doer. In 1913 the firm did 41 million dollars' worth of business. In 1916, the year after he took over as president, they did 61 million.

The plants were huge, but still not big enough to take care of all the orders for cars the public needed. War orders cut down on car production. In 1916 Erskine had his engineers design a modern plant for car-making. South Bend feared the new president would take the company away from South Bend. But Erskine assured J.M. person-ally that the new plant would be built on the home grounds, and that some time in the future the Detroit plant would be brought to South Bend. The company had paid off all bank loans and was paying out dividends on a 10 per cent basis.

The new plant would be able to turn out 700 cars a day. Three times the number the Detroit plant could make. On December 12, 1916, ground was broken for the new forge, machine, and power plants.

MEANWHILE, America was being drawn into the war. President Wilson, who had been re-elected with the slogan,

"We are too proud to fight," now felt the balance of power was needed to defeat the Germans moving quickly to become a master race over a slave world. England had lost the best manhood of two generations, the French were sunk down under great losses. Russia was staggering under greed, corruption, and moronic rulers. The German U-boats were sinking neutral American shipping, sending women and children to the bottom with a disregard, as usual, of any humane ideals.

The Germans offered Mexico three Southwestern states if they would come in against us and let Mexico be used as a jumping-off spot for a German invasion.

In February, 1917, Wilson broke off diplomatic relations with Germany. By April we were in our first World War.

WORLD WAR I

Would the last of the Studebaker brothers—solid but old—live to see his country enter World War I? On January 3, 1917, he and Mary had celebrated their fifty-seventh wedding anniversary. They were almost retired now to their Sunnyside estate, with their great Danes and Shetland ponies. John Mohler had shared some of his wealth with the public. He and his brothers had endowed hospital rooms, given South Bend a Y.M.C.A., a park fountain, and built two churches. Now he rested, and waited . . .

On March 17, the South Bend *Saturday Tribune* had a headline that now appears ironic:

RUSSIA BECOMES LARGEST REPUBLIC IN THE WORLD

But the right-hand important column on the front page held this special story:

DEATH CLAIMS LAST OF FIVE BIG BROTHERS
J.M. STUDEBAKER, SR., PASSES AWAY IN
MIDST OF FAMILY.
END WAS VERY PEACEFUL.
MANUFACTURER AND PHILANTHROPIST,
CONSCIOUS TO LAST, DISCUSSES BUSINESS ALMOST
UP TO FINAL HOUR.

The world had changed, had changed a lot, and would go on changing. The war was on and it had to be won. The women of South Bend rolled bandages and looked very romantic in their Red Cross hoods. The cars late at night passed the people rocking on their porches, young voices buzzing in excitement at this turn in world affairs that was forcing America to "make the world safe for democracy." It was a good slogan and it came from the heart. But slogans didn't win wars. The American machine for making war was untested. It had paraded in the last of the Indian posts, had chased Mexican bandits on horseback. Football was famous at West Point, but did it contain new Grants and Lees, better Shermans and Stonewall Jacksons? The truth was the American war machine had been rusting since the Civil War (the Spanish-American War seemed to be merely Teddy Roosevelt's private fray). It was beginning to polish itself for battle.

South Bend went to war. Boys from South Bend, and elsewhere, marched off to France, singing "Over There," and "Beautiful Katie." At South Bend the plants hummed, turning out gun carriages, artillery wheels, shell parts, and shell adapters. Escort wagons, excavators, oilers, tank wagons, and ambulances rolled from the gates. They also made harness, cavalry bridles, and bayonet scabbards.

Erskine cut down the number of civilian cars by half, and at the Detroit plant, a $300,000 building was added for government orders.

But the new postwar cars to come were on Erskine's mind. He ordered the engineers to design a whole new line of cars for after the war. On their drawing boards appeared light and heavy cars, trucks, and commercial models. As the war ended, new models were shipped to Buffalo. They were driven to Albany, then to Montreal, to Quebec and down across New York, Pennsylvania, through Ohio and Michigan. It was a tough long run of over 20,000 miles over the worst roads, in the worst weather. At the end of the year the cars were running a continuous 30,000 miles around a Chicago speedway. After a full check-over and analysis, Erskine ordered them into limited production. In January, 1918, the cars were exhibited in the New York auto show. The Light Six, the Special Six, and the Big Six were the popular cars of the show.

WARREN GAMALIEL HARDING sat in the White House and the Treaty of Versailles was written, leaving, many felt, too much of the wrong kind of thinking alive in Germany. In America, Erskine studied the high cost of living and tried to get more people to buy more cars. He got on well with the workers. He set up a central management committee to review the discharge of any employee. Good labor relations were always a proud point at Studebaker, and Erskine believed in them. His broad new program for workers was a good one. An anniversary bonus for every worker, stock purchase rights, graduated vacations with pay, retirement pensions, and group insurance. And organized recreational programs. This was all pretty radical in 1919. But it paid off, as his labor turnover that year was only a fifth of that of some other firms.

Erskine got rid of the carriage and wagon business. Cars were the future. Wagons and gear were liquidated gradually. Also, the Detroit plant would be moved soon to South Bend. And a new Light Six would be designed. A quality car in a low-price field. New plants went up in South Bend. Bigger building programs than ever. Sales had jumped from 39,000 units in 1919 to 51,000 units in 1920.

In 1922, *Barrons Magazine*, in their "Men in Wall Street's Eye," gave him a special section. Sales had just reached $133 million. "We eat obstacles for breakfast," Erskine told the reporters.

Nineteen hundred and twenty-six saw the last of the Detroit plant moved to South Bend. Harold S. Vance, vice-president in charge of production and engineering, was in charge of the move. And Paul Hoffman, Studebaker's most successful distributor and dealer, had come to South Bend the previous year, as vice-president in charge of sales. A modern engineering and research plant was set up. And a laboratory using the latest scientific methods. Then an 800-acre proving ground was laid out outside of town where special roads and tracks and grades reproduced every condition and hazard that could overtake a car. Here every model was tested for months; discarded were those that could not stand up to Studebaker standards for automotive perfection.

That year Studebaker introduced a new small car called the Erskine Six. Not in South Bend or New York. But in Paris. Europe was mad about small cars, with their small use of gas as an added attraction. The car was also shown in London. Twenty-six thousand cars were sold abroad. It did well in America, too.

Nineteen twenty-seven was a tough year, not because people didn't have money, the stock market was climbing, but because of high-production costs and heavy costs of introducing new large models such as the President Eight.

On the second of January, there was held a diamond jubilee dinner for 1,800 guests. Erskine was still busy, planning and traveling, speaking and producing. In 1928 the company bought a substantial share of the stock of the Pierce-Arrow Motor Car Company of Buffalo. A larger Erskine Six would be brought out; and Studebaker, Erskine proudly said, "now blanketed the motor car field with a line of passenger cars from the Erskine, the Studebaker, to the Pierce-Arrow." The firm had "something for everyone," in any price range.

THE ROARING TWENTIES

There were a few horses still left, in fact a horse and wagon was blown to bits when a bomb was left in front of J.P. Morgan's on Wall Street. But mostly one traveled by car, by train, and by plane. It was to be a decade of changes, not just at Studebaker. The flapper had come to be the most popular kind of girl with her short skirts, rolled stockings, shingled head, and her boy friend with a raccoon coat and pocket flask. "The Great Experiment" was on to do away with drinking, and everybody knew someone called Tony who had one eye built into a door and sold stuff "right off the boat — yeah, scraped off!"

The morals and manners of the time of the buggy and the first horseless carriage were in for a shock. Studebaker roadsters stood in front of frat houses at Princeton, and carried the million-dollar gate to the Dempsey-Firpo fight in Jersey City. Little Caesars took people "for a ride" in motor cars. Will Rogers warned us with his wit.

Car colors went to fire-house red and electric blue, and solid disc wheels took over from wooden spokes, and then wire wheels were made at South Bend to carry the Sunday mobs over the new highways being built.

One of the success stories of South Bend in the twenties was that of a bright young man in the sales department of Studebaker. John Cavanaugh, everyone said, would go far. It was a company of young men under Erskine. Fred Fish would retire in time, and bright young men like John Cavanaugh would be the future of the company, with Paul Hoffman and Harold Vance.

Cavanaugh did his job better than expected and in the sales department showed what his hard work, his brilliant mind, was able to project into the Studebaker selling ideas. But he was not fully happy. There was, he felt, for him, some higher calling, a more humble approach to this world, a stronger service that a man could give to people.

He spoke to Harold Vance. "I am leaving the company."

"But why?"

"I have felt a call. I am going to study to become a priest."

"If you feel that way, I suppose you must."

"I feel I must."

"But if you find you've been wrong about your call, you come back to us."

So John Cavanaugh studied for the priesthood, answered his call to grace, went with his faith in his mission through the long course of his desire. But he was put into no cloistered cell. In time he became the brilliant president of Notre Dame University. He remained there until retired in 1952, the head of the great school, looking across his campus, when he wasn't too busy, to where the chimneys of Studebaker smudged the horizon. He had chosen between two ways of life. He remained friends with the people at the plants. And Harold Vance, not a Catholic and tagged by an earlier president as "my favorite heretic," served on the Notre Dame board with him.

THE EXPANSION frenzy and stock-buying held the entire nation in those years of the twenties. Stocks were climbing, more and more people were investing in the market. Prices for stocks were at an all-time high. The Studebaker brothers from 1868 to 1911 had shown $16.7 million in earned profits for the company, of which only $6.8 millions were paid in dividends. But in the twenties — years of the big bull market — these were piker figures.

In 1924 Studebaker dividends amounted to 59 per cent of the profits. In 1929, they were up to the incredible figure of nearly 90 per cent. These were boom times, Erskine said, and everyone in the world agreed. He was honestly bullish on America. He would not sell his country short. The future belonged to all America, he felt. To Studebaker, to the workers in the plants, to the people riding around in their good cars on a fine day in June. The company had expanded its sales list to 50 models. The stock market continued to rise. The weather passed into Indian summer. People drove out into the country, among the ripe corn. Fall came, the elm leaves fell, the sugar maples turned red and golden and then brown . . . August, September . . . the fall would be a rich time and a good time, and the people no longer jacked up their cars for the winter and let the air out of their tires. Football would be here soon, the great teams and the packed stands, and driving a car over the roads of fall with a crisp chill in the air. It was good to be alive in America in 1929, in October . . .

STUDEBAKER was part of this booming picture, and its leaders were no more aware than the rest of the world that a cold wind was rising, that history had taken a sudden turn for the worse.

WALL STREET LAYS EGG!

(HEADLINE IN **VARIETY**, OCTOBER, 1929)

Studebaker in its eventful history had been weaned on panics and depressions. It had tossed off and weathered the big ones in the seventies and nineties, the lulu of 1907, the postwar depression of 1920. It had learned how to roll with the punch, and with clever footwork to keep fighting until times got better. Times always did get better, their records showed.

But 1929 was a special depression, king-size. It was bigger, deeper, wider than any that had yet hit a young and growing country. It was a deep belly cramp, and it would take time to straighten out. Erskine and his staff at South Bend were busy as usual when the stock market of 1929 fell apart. Hoffman and Vance looked at the reports and shook their heads. This was going to be a bad one.

Erskine had full faith in his ideas for business as usual. The cure for a falling market was a good new small car. The Studebaker Light Six had pulled them out of the postwar slump. Expansion, he decided, would take up the slack of the depression, the fall of the market. So a new low-price car was on order. The designers sat down at their drawing boards and went to work. They produced the Rockne Six. Sales were dropping off as the year ended, jobs were hard to get, prices were way down. Erskine felt the prices of stocks were not always in true relationship to the real condition of business. Too many people had gone into unhealthy speculation and had forced up stock prices. Now the wind and water were being pressed out of the stocks and they would level off to some real relationship to the true state of affairs. Orders continued to drop. There were lay-offs at Studebaker, wages were cut. By October, 1930, four million people in the nation were unemployed. It was no longer just a "stock market readjustment." By 1932 eleven million people were unemployed. The White House sat firm. It was "against a direct or indirect dole." Americans didn't take handouts. "Prosperity was just around the corner." Why not two Rocknes in every garage?

In 1931, nineteen important nations had gone off the gold standard. In the election of 1932, Hoover said, "grass would grow in the streets," if his party did not win. Banks closed their doors after election day, big solid banks. Erskine held firm to his principles. He believed in his country, his company, his job, and his cars. Studebaker had gone on making better cars. In 1931 it introduced "free wheeling" in a new line of cars. Sales dropped but Erskine no longer expected things to be like the boom days. Things would level off. The stock of the company *must* remain solid and healthy. He had the directors declare a dividend of $2,800,000. This cost capital but it kept Studebaker stock at blue-chip level. Erskine was a man of figures, of bookkeeping. Stock prices had special value to him, and those values must be kept up for the stockholders, for those who believed in Studebaker. Next year all salaries were cut again . . .

The new light car would bring back business, Erskine said. The car was a good one. The Rockne Six was well engineered, well built. It was also low-priced. But even that price was too much for a nation selling apples at street corners. Nevertheless, Erskine still believed the new car would bring back business.

The depression continued. People were hopeful for the future, but the good times were slow in coming back. Working capital was shrunk. Losses and expenditures went on. The South Bend factory worked part time.

ERSKINE was more active than ever. Now was a time for mergers. Now was a time for good, solid firms to get together. The White Motor Company made fine trucks. It had a good working capital. Why not combine the two firms? Erskine, in the name of Studebaker, acquired 95 per cent of all White common stock.

It was a practical thing. It would merge two great names, it would make them stronger together. But a minority group in White said no . . . unless Studebaker wanted to buy above the market price and in cash. Also, White was an Ohio corporation. There was a state law forbidding an Ohio company from being merged with an out-of-state company and sharing its working capital with that company.

STUDEBAKER assets still stood solid in South Bend. There was a huge stock of finished cars. It had loyal salesmen, stock piles, it had skilled men, fine men, wise men. Nothing much had changed from the boom years, only times were too bad to sell cars. They owed the banks $6 million.

On March 18, 1933, the wise thing to do was to reorganize, in receivership. Studebaker had licked a lot of panics and depressions before and it would lick this one. If reorganization was the way to do it, Studebaker would do it this way. The New Deal sat in Washington, things were done in new ways now. Stock deals, promotion methods, were changing. The New Deal had its own philosophy of business. Change was in the air and there were new stock market laws and new security procedures.

Albert Russel Erskine didn't do things that way. He belonged to an older, different school. He moved out of his office and went home. Three months later he was dead.

STUDEBAKER still stood out against the South Bend sky. It existed in its plants, its stock, and its men in charge. Harold Vance, Paul Hoffman, and Ashton G. Bean of the White Motor Company, took over as receivers . . . took over for the 16,000 families in factories and in salesrooms who were Studebaker. They still had current assets of $7 million. They were an operating concern, with a big stock of finished cars on hand. Dealers and workers were loyal. However, the bank holidays of the New Deal had frozen the usual credit lines. But they would carry on and make cars.

Harold Vance and Paul Hoffman had newspapers carry a national coast-to-coast ad for Studebaker:

> Studebaker carries on . . . Studebaker is still Studebaker in spirit, scope, and service. There has been no change except for the better, in the policies and programs of the historic Studebaker Institution. . . .
>
> The great South Bend plants of Studebaker, closed since the announcement of the bank moratorium, reopen Tuesday, March 21, under the direction of . . . seasoned automotive executives.
>
> This pioneering organization has already faced and fought and triumphed over more "depressions," wars and "bad times" than any other company in the automobile business.
>
> Studebaker now confidently carries on, assured that it can continue to offer the American public the kind of automobiles and service for which the Studebaker name is distinguished.

THE HARD WAY

Harold Vance and Paul Hoffman showed practical results quickly in reorganization. During the first full month
of operation 3,806 cars were sold. They showed a small
profit of $20,000.

It was decided — on this cheerful note — to get money
to retool for new models.

FOR OVER 20 years Harold Vance and Paul Hoffman had
been part of Studebaker. Now they discovered that en-
tirely on their shoulders rested the vast company's future.
They were in charge, fully in charge, and if it continued
to function they would have to make it work. They would
have to handle distributors, production, sales, auditors,
and bankers. All the problems of raw materials, and the
finished products. *And* the bankers.

By December, 1933, the firm was showing a profit of
$54,000 and had 224 new Studebaker dealers. They also
had their White Motor Company stock. Their working
capital was $5,757,000. Hoffman went to Washington to
see how the new Securities Act would affect their reorganization. To stay within the changing securities law was
the problem if they were to get underwriters' backing for
the retooling of the new models. Hoffman did a good job.

It was at this time he laid the groundwork for, without knowing it, himself entering the government.

Refinancing would have to be worked out in New York. And Hoffman and Vance spent a great deal of their lives on trains and planes between South Bend and New York. Lehman Brothers, early Studebaker bankers, and some other investment houses, now agreed to underwrite $6,800,000 of new securities for Studebaker — *if* Vance and Hoffman could get extra underwriting for part of that amount themselves. It was not easy. The country was still shaking from its rattling ride on the depression train. Money was still tight, and no one knew for sure the true state of the auto market. Vance and Hoffman went from door to door on Wall Street, showing their statements, their sales charts, their production figures. They did it, but it wasn't easy. They still wonder today how they had the perseverance to keep going until the whole amount was underwritten. Maybe because there wasn't any other way.

Their last $200,000 came from Ernest Woodruff, who turned out to be an old friend of John Mohler and an admirer of the Studebaker brothers.

"I knew J.M. Put me down," he said.

The country was about to see a miracle. Of the hundreds of fine and old auto firms, few had been able to stay in business past the wild youth of the business. *None* — not one auto company had ever come through receivership successfully!

The triumph of Studebaker was the victory of the eldest and foremost maker of American highway transportation to recover and go on selling wheels and quality to a nation it had grown up with.

To do this in the strong relentless competition of the auto industry — the coldest, toughest in the world — meant something. It was not easy, it was not a job for weaklings — and it was done.

The full reorganization plans were approved, and on March 9, 1935, the cash was turned over to Studebaker. South Bend was again solidly in business as a maker of cars. Now all they had to do was to produce and sell their new cars. The closely knit sales and production team worked hard, worked night and day. America had developed depression-bred buying habits and new car demands, and they had to meet them, and quickly. What the nation now wanted was good transportation, at a price. There were millions of old Studebaker customers and a car had to be created that would give them the quality of the old-time cars with the economy and styling of the new demands. It was a test for free enterprise, and the team at South Bend went ahead to meet it.

At a meeting of trade executives at Northwestern University, Paul Hoffman explained the new problems in American production:

> . . . to sum it all up . . . business has a two-fold job if it is to play its part in saving free enterprise. . . . We must fight those minority groups who are willing to sell out free enterprise by seeking government help in the form of price production controls or licensing laws. . . . In the field of labor, we must cease defending all employers and condemning all labor leaders and begin to use discrimination.

Meanwhile, the Studebaker Champion had been put onto drawing boards, engineers were at work on the new car. From 1935 to 1939, a vast group of designers and mechanics with the know-how of car engineering and designing were at work on the Champion. Tests were made of parts, motors, and performances. New designs appeared: climatizers, hill holders, rotary door latches, planar suspension for better stabilization. Less weight, more car, lower operating costs. On the company testing grounds, car after car was worn out in detailed, grueling tests. The finished car, when it hit the market, had to be worthy. It had been a time of sweating it out at South Bend. Twelve hundred parts-makers and suppliers had to be geared into the new production plans. The raw materials, glass, and metal molders, foundries from 34 states had to be merged to make a better car.

It was not all designing and processing. There was also an important item listed as *labor*. Times had changed. Labor was organizing, was demanding and bargaining. A.F. of L. labor under the Blue Eagle was now drifting into the newer, more aggressive C.I.O. Workers demanded a union contract at Studebaker. Hoffman and Vance told them to work out their contract and bring it in. The firm's leaders made it clear they were not against organization, but they also spoke of their position after reorganization, their plans and what they had ahead of them before the new car would be in the salesroom. The new contract was drawn up and signed. Studebaker's record of never having a major labor disturbance continued.

Labor strife that beset the auto industry in the thirties left Studebaker unscathed. As Harold Vance explained it to the author of this book, the almost complete unionization of the South Bend working force contributed to this happy state of affairs. Paradoxically, plants where only minorities of the workers belonged to unions often found themselves faced with strikes and walkouts.

What Studebaker management saw, and others failed to grasp, was that where unionization was unopposed, even encouraged, then the union membership became truly representative of all the workers, and that when all the workers of a plant are taken together the majority are level-headed and approach all problems with a common-sense attitude. In plants where unionization was opposed by management, the level-headed, common-sense majority stayed out of the unions, leaving them to the control and direction of the radical fringe which exists in all plants. Plants where radical minorities controlled the labor organizations soon were in hot water. Not so at Studebaker where because union membership included *all* workers, union affairs were in the hands of the level-headed majority.

Many men who work at Studebaker are men whose fathers had worked there or still work there. Fathers taught their sons their special jobs. Three generations in the plants are not rare. The average age of a worker at Studebaker went up for this reason. In 1923 it was 32 years, in 1940 forty-four years. The average length of service of a Studebaker worker was close to 11 years.

Vance and Hoffman knew people, and the human factor in auto-making. And they weren't afraid to say it in public.

AMERICA was never to be the same after the great depression. The wild, free days of catch-as-catch-can enterprise were over. Vance and Hoffman knew it. They knew there would be other rainy days ahead in the future. The nation knew it. Its memory was sharp with the image of the Dust Bowl acres blowing to hell-and-gone, and the car, the family car, cut down and piled with bedding and kids and the last of the farm products. And heading West in despair. Where John Mohler and the gold hunters had marched, singing to fiddle music, the sharecroppers and the Okies had gone along Highway 66 with the last strength of their cars, looking for something to eat, something to lift and pick for a handout to feed the kids.

The new managers remembered those days when the Studebakers on the road were old, but still going, and the horizon held little hope for their one-time customers. They remembered the shabby lines in the city streets. The hard eyes in the faces of the white-collar workers, the worry in the middle-class streets where the sons were taken from college. Where daughters gave up their music lessons, and the hired girl was sent away. Harold Vance and Paul Hoffman had been through it, had come through with the company and there was scar tissue on their emotions, their outlook, just as there was on every American who had known the lean years of the boys in the C.C.C. camps, the shovels of the W.P.A., the halls of the Federal Theater and the Federal Art projects. It hadn't been a special depression for one class; there had been enough misery to go around for everyone—from the crash of Insull's empire to the sharecropper who couldn't feed a mule to raise cotton he couldn't sell.

Vance and Hoffman knew that figures and charts came down to real people. People you could touch and talk to. And cars were not to them just items on production sheets; they were things people bought and owned, used and repaired—and added up as part of their assets in life.

THE CHAMPION IS BORN

Over the years, as Harold Sines Vance came into his own in the Studebaker Corporation, he welded his personal future firmly to that of the firm and the cars it made.

Port Huron, Michigan, where he grew up, was important to its citizens and there was talk of progress as the century, brand new and excited by the motor car, advanced into its first decade.

People used to the hunting rifle, the lake boats, the art of farm reapers and binders, took with skill to the newer business of making machines. Port Huron was proud of several factories — among them the E-M-F machine shops where parts for some of the first autos of the new century were being made. Here, Harold Vance became a mechanic's apprentice at the wage of 15 cents an hour. The making of a motor car was, he found out, an intricate and involved process. Before the days of assembly line production, before special processes and materials were to be had by lifting a phone, the young man found that motor-car-making was a job for craftsmen — the delight of the Yankee mechanics filing and fitting each part into place with care.

Harold Vance did not stay very long as a mechanic's apprentice. Studebaker had absorbed E-M-F.

The auto plants of Studebaker first in Detroit and Port Huron were separate units from the wagon works in South Bend. Harold Vance worked hard at the auto-making, but the wagon was still king at South Bend.

In his rise in company ranks from assistant treasurer, through the purchasing department and as a production executive, Harold Vance saw the motor car's popularity overtake the wagon and the gates at South Bend open wide for the new hero, the motor car. When Studebaker moved its auto plants to the home grounds, it was Harold Vance who moved them.

In 1918 he had gone over to Bethlehem Steel as a production engineer. With peace returning and new models to put into production at South Bend, Vance went back with the old firm at South Bend as assistant to the president. He had come a long way since 1910 and had learned a lot about steel, motors, and production. In 1922 two important things happened to the boy from Port Huron. On June 17, 1922, he married Agnes M. Monaghan. He also became export sales manager. A year later he was general sales manager for Studebaker.

In 1926 he was elected vice-president in charge of production and engineering; things were humming and that same year he was elected to the membership of the board of directors of The Studebaker Corporation.

The photographs of the period in the plant's history show him a young man with firm features and humorous eyes.

WHEN THE depression came it was Harold Vance, with Paul Hoffman, who successfully carried out the reorganization of Studebaker, and when it became effective in 1935, they became chairman of the board and president, respectively, joint managers of The Studebaker Corporation.

When Hoffman went to Washington, Vance, remaining as chairman of the board, assumed the duties of president. His is a hard, full-time job in an industry of competing giants, shifting world values, and national tensions. In the old office where John M. Studebaker, Fish, and Erskine (their paintings stare down on him), once held power, behind one of the old desks, Harold Vance faces the problems of his times and of Studebaker.

WHEN THE author of this book talked with Harold Vance, he admitted concern about the way the world was going, and Studebaker's place in that world.

It's a changed world. Times are different. A hundred years ago people thought they were sure what the future would be. We no longer know or even think we know, and so Studebaker is geared to continue no matter what happens. We are car-makers, we are producers of transportation. As independents in a tough field we work to produce a car at a price with no loss of quality. Like John Mohler, we go out personally and test what goes into the products: only it's no longer just seasoned wood.

We plan for the future, but we don't play recklessly, and we don't want to experiment with every gadget someone thinks of adding to a car; when it's been tested and approved of, you'll find it on your Studebaker. That's the way the brothers did business, that's the way we try to do business.

Our business is making cars. We have big plans for the future. Everything we do here is geared to future plans . . . The car of the future? The Studebaker we intend to make will be a lot like the cars we have already made, although I see many changes. It will be stronger, more beautiful, more comfortable to ride in and drive, and will contain whatever new advances have been proven on our testing grounds.

But what will always remain will be the same desire to give quality just a little beyond the expectation of the buyer.

VANCE cannot taste or fully picture the future, but he faces it every day at that old desk, and he faces it calmly, confident, and ready, with the same humorous twinkle in his eyes that saw it all when the Studebaker car was a pup.

The century of promise has become in many ways the century of wars for human decency and survival. Studebaker, Harold Vance as Studebaker, South Bend, Indiana, and Main Street, U.S.A., in many ways typify the special virtues of the century as they flex their home-grown muscles and do their jobs, sure of their know-how and what they are working to keep, protect, and pass on to their kids.

THE CHAMPION was a successful car. A very successful car. The gleaming new cars rolled out of the plant. The sales figures rose. The company was fully healthy again, and the team that ran it watched it closely, took its pulse often, and rarely relaxed. For, of most of the early names in automobile history, Studebaker was one of the few that remained. Many good old names were gone, remembered only in legends or songs. The Stutz Bearcat, the Maxwell, the Franklin, many of the road heroes of the last half-century. But Studebaker was back on top.

The success of the Champion was rooted in the grasp that Studebaker management had of the transportation problems and needs of the nations. And, as invariably happens when a business enterprise correctly assays the needs of the public, and acts intelligently on its findings, the reaction was specific, immediate, and profitable.

As Harold Vance explains it, the reasons for Studebaker's entry into the low-price field with the Champion in 1939 were more fundamental than the desire to increase the sales and profits of the company. In fact, some top-level people in the company weren't sure that the car would be a financial success.

> Yes [he recalls], some thought we were taking a risk. A lot of our ready capital went into development of that car. But we didn't think a low-price car had to be a low-quality car. If that had been true, we wouldn't have built it. For 90 years Studebaker had never offered the customer less than the best for his money, and we didn't change with the Champion. Going into the low-price field was plain good business, in 1939 and for the long pull. We couldn't ignore the tremendous need for low-cost transportation. We decided the public wanted it, and the people with foresight in our business would give it to them. Low price meant high volume, and volume is the priceless ingredient of growth.
>
> Most of us felt the Champion was the best investment we could possibly make against risk in the future. We had a loyal body of Studebaker owners. What we set out to do, and did, was to expand that number of owners as fast as possible, keeping both the old and new owners loyal, with a quality car the average family could afford to buy. We believed the low-price car was the answer to the transportation needs of the country and that we ought to build it. It was as simple as that.

Simple and successful. The Champion was introduced in 1939, and sales that year were almost double those of 1938. Now there was no doubt. Studebaker had come back. There was new breath and hope as well as courage at South Bend. Days of progress and expansion and development lay ahead.

ONLY THE Germans were stirring again, and in the fall of 1939 Hitler marched into Poland. The flames were lit

again in the war lamps of the world. A special session of
Congress annulled the Neutrality Act. Harold Vance and
Paul Hoffman were in Washington again; the news was:
car production for civilian use would be cut. Steel was to
be a sword again . . .

Vance and Knudsen in Washington talked it over.
They were for spending the major parts of funds appro-
priated by Congress for defense to create capacity to produce war material rather than to produce material itself—
their views prevailed—we got the plants built and
equipped so that when Pearl Harbor put us into the war
we were quickly able to produce planes and guns and all
the hardware which modern war requires.

THE 1942 MODEL was big news the day it was put on curtailed production. The new Studebaker car got a big
send-off, but orders could not be filled. It would have to
wait for the war's end for the full-production green light.

On the Burma Road thousands of trucks did the killing
tearing thousands of miles, with full loads, into China.
Studebaker had 5,000 dusty trucks on the road making the
trip. The Chinese Red Cross was all Studebaker-equipped.
Soon South Bend was making only trucks and aviation
engines. More trucks rushed more supplies to the ocean
transports. Studebaker went on making trucks. Studebaker
built bigger plants, and more trucks rolled out. South
Bend now made aircraft engines, too.

IT WAS NOT an easy conversion to make but it was a
famous one. The men behind it did not stint of their time
or effort. They must reach peak production, almost at
once, of war orders which eventually totaled $1,200,000,-
000. It was not just pressing buttons and hiring more
help. An airplane engine had 45,000 machine operations
and had to be inspected 50,000 times. It had taken four

years' time and $4 million to produce the Champion in peacetime. Now they had to switch over to airplane engines at a short notice. . . . New dies, tools, and methods had to be created overnight. New techniques had to be invented. Harold Vance and his plantmen coordinated the job and got it rolling. Paul Hoffman toured the auto plants in Detroit, talking cooperation of efforts and ideas. He put it on the barrelhead. We had nothing to lose if we didn't but our world.

There are those who suggest that if we are to accomplish this task we must give up our freedom and submit to dictatorship. If I believed that to be true, I'd say "Amen," but it so happens that it's a doctrine I utterly reject. I believe with all my heart and soul that free management and free labor, each doing its part of the job, but cooperating with each other and with government, can outproduce any economy in which labor is enslaved and management shackled.

The company stripped for action. It looked good and able. Sales had climbed from $43 million in 1938 to $84 million in 1940. By 1941 — with the problems of conversion and curtailed car sales — 133,855 units, selling for $115,-700,000 — had been moved at a profit of $2,400,000. By 1943, geared for war production, a sales record of $364,-100,000 had been set, and the first dividend since the reorganization — 25 cents a share — had been paid.

THE DESPERATE war years rolled on. Every part of the world was on fire. Enemy cities and rivers and factories were torn in fury from the earth with bombs carried by planes powered by engines made in South Bend.

In the gray, grim convoys across the ice belts of the world Studebaker trucks by the hundreds of thousands were moving toward the battered battlelines of our Allies. Two hundred and ninety thousand trucks and parts were sent into Allied hands and helped turn the Battle of Europe in our favor. It was a time of taking help where we found it, and, as the mud and dust of *Mittel Europa* ground under the wheels of troop-and-gun-carrying Studebakers, there arose in the hearts of Americans the hope that the war would be won soon and that peace would come for all times.

Studebaker engineers at South Bend designed and built for the armed forces a tracked vehicle called "The Weasel" that would float over the boggy shores of the South Seas or across the winter snows of Europe and carry Americans into battle just a little better than before. The trucks poured out, as usual—and the plane engines.

STRANGERS in odd uniforms and speaking far-off tongues came to South Bend. It was one of the showplaces where our Allies were encouraged and shown in person the power and punch behind all our war efforts.

TWENTY-TWO

THE POSTWAR WORLD

In 1944 the only measuring rod of effort at South Bend was the production volume. Then at last the agony was over. The war was won. Europe rested from its effort and torment. The atom bomb had fallen on Japan and filled the dreams of the world. The factories that had worked on it knew they had worked well. The Jap gave up and bowed and signed his surrender. Tropical islands became sacred names in Marine, Navy, and Army history.

Reconversion showed on the balance sheets of 1945. Sales dipped to $212,800,000. Profits were $3,200,000. War contracts terminated. The auto came back from its drawing boards and company files. Now Studebaker was back in business for the American family. Working capital in 1946 was $33,600,000. Its inventories were around $13,500,000, and plants and equipment were assets valued at $17,700,000.

It was not easy to convert to cars in the mixed world of 1946. War was ended, but the pain and confusion continued for a while. Strikes in suppliers' plants held production of the new car down to 119,275 units. It was a new car all over, with its daring design that was the target so often that year of the nation's cartoonists and wits that it helped set up Studebaker cars as something different and special in the automobile business.

It fitted in with our new frontiers of a rising birth rate, an older population, growing national income (and taxes), and was an example of the business discharging its responsibilities to a nation hungry for machines of peace.

The car sold well and plant capacity expanded.

IN APRIL, 1948, Paul Hoffman became head of the Economic Cooperation Administration, directing the Marshall Plan, resigning as president of Studebaker to take the job. Harold Vance, who had come a long way from the Port Huron factory in 1910 took over as president as well as chairman of the board. He and the company's directors set a definite plan—still going on—for the growth and expansion of Studebaker.

He became sole head of one of the oldest, most powerful manufacturing and selling organizations in American history. In five years sales had risen from 1947's $268 million for 191,531 autos, trucks, parts, and accessories to over a half-billion dollars in 1951. Sales in 1948 mounted to $383 million, and to $473 million in 1949. A 99-year record was set in 1950 when 334,554 autos and trucks were sold and total sales volume was $477 million.

A new truck plant was put in operation and the foundry expanded.

Government restrictions on production in 1951 reduced unit production in Studebaker's one hundredth year to approximately 285,000 units but dollar volume, including income from defense contracts, was more than $503 million—the first time that sales crossed the half-billion-dollar mark, and approximately one million times the sales of the Studebaker enterprise in its first year of operation, 1852.

There were dark clouds on the horizon, and Harold Vance did not let himself go in the expansive hell-for-leather frenzy of the days of A.R. Erskine.

THE STUDEBAKER plants themselves at South Bend are an amazing history of one hundred years of factory styling and design. Great new banks of factory forms, as modern as a Picasso painting, stand cheek-by-jowl with red brick plants that recall side whiskers of the Civil War and the cigars of General Grant. Modern foundries that amaze the world with their continual melting furnaces and vats and pouring trolleys stand close to tool sheds and brick towers that remembered the Rough Riders and company picnics in peg-topped pants. The grounds in South Bend have a flavor. They have somehow never lost the sound and mood of the wagon forges of the Studebaker brothers, and yet are marching in the forefront of scientific progress with the best the world of science and new laboratory methods have to offer.

The foundry is one of the wonders of the steel and casting business. Under its great vaulting roofs, furnaces pour their white-hot molten steel into round, rotating vats. These vats are tilted, when they are needed, into high, traveling containers running on overhead rails that pour directly into a battery of moving engine molds. The engine castings are cooled and moved onto a new assembly line, one of the longest and newest in the auto industry. Here the new V-8 engine blocks move past drills, planes, and tools that bore and polish and measure, and then an automatic device turns them over for work on both sides. Where over 100 men once slowly handled the engine blocks, the new assembly line is run by two men at button controls. At the last drilling, as bolt-holes are placed in the engine blocks, they are lifted to a new line to have pistons, shafts, and other parts put in place. Still moving, the engine is built up, part by part. Carburetors, water pumps, many other components.

Then moving to rows of testing blocks the new engine is put through its paces. The engine then goes to the assembly plant where it is installed in the chassis. Meanwhile, in other departments of the plant, the steel forms of fenders, hood, and body have been assembled and finished. Placed on a moving platform, the car body and fenders are inspected, rough spots ground down. Sprayed several times with rust-protecting solutions and surfaced to take the paint, the body moves slowly through the paint-spraying and paint-baking room. After the first coats, the final enamel is sprayed on and the body inspected again. Now, on a new moving section, craftsmen skillfully and swiftly fill the empty body with wiring, light outlets, special safety-glass windows. Dashboards, windshield wipers, head and tail lights, whole units for doorlocks and other sections, all prepared and waiting, go into place as the body moves slowly past armies of workers. Inspected after every operation, the upholstery, the bumpers, the view mirrors, the final knobs, and the chrome finish are put in place, and the body is ready to be moved and joined to the chassis on the final assembly line.

From the start of assembly, special slips go with every car, on which are checked off every item attached to the still-building car. The slip contains not only the optional items and details being put into the individual car but also the local dealer's name who had ordered the car, where and how it is to be shipped. Still moving, the car is put through a heavy rain storm of special shower pipes. A man inside the car checks its water-proofing. Then battery, tires, oil, and gas are added and the car is run by testing crews, lights switched on, locks given a last test. Then, its windows washed, its chrome protected, it moves toward the great auto carriers or the waiting freight car.

Each movement, from prebuilt parts to finished car, from the spot welders who put together the stamped steel sheet forms, to the women who, at sewing machines, sew together the upholstery, every action is scientific in its accuracy for speed and for quality.

The men and women of Studebaker are paid higher than average auto industries pay. Seasoned men along the production line showed the author how springs, small parts, and special fittings are put together. Many of these craftsmen had been over forty years with Studebaker.

Each car model is a new problem solved, some detail improved, some action redesigned. . . . But the method of work and the quality of the work are old stories at South Bend. The raw steel, the rubber and nylon, the wires and glass, take shape. What had been a few hours ago hundreds of products becomes just one thing: a modern motor car.

THE FIRM has always been strong in overseas markets. But these markets now are changed. Frozen funds keep the buyers of Studebaker products from buying as they did in the old days—but still the products of South Bend go to India, to South Africa, and into whatever country in free Europe can still manage to pay for a bill-of-lading.

The United States, Alaska, and Hawaii are served by an organization of 19 regional branches, 24 parts-depots, and almost 3,000 dealers keyed in with the home offices. In Hamilton, Ontario, Studebaker owns a Canadian subsidiary where cars and trucks are assembled for home use and for export. Abroad, there are 11 distributor-owned assembly plants, and 1,500 sales outlets.

Vance and his staff are a team ready to produce a car, convert to defense, to turn from wheels to jet engines at the flash of an order. And do.

Studebaker's business is the making of the wheels that carry the American families and the Americans' products over the face of the earth. But they keep in step with the world as it is — not as it might be. In the annual report for 1951 Harold Vance expressed it best:

> Our policy continues to be that we shall devote our resources in plants, skills, and otherwise, wholeheartedly to the defense production assignments which have been given us and, at the same time, that we shall produce all of the Studebaker cars and trucks which the government will permit.
>
> The present directors, managers, and employees of Studebaker look back over the history of the first hundred years, and find therein a reason for some proper amount of pride over what has been done, but, much more importantly, they find a great encouragement for what lies ahead, for what may be done in the second hundred years of Studebaker's history.

This was a true echo of what old John Mohler Studebaker himself said fifty years before, when Studebaker had reached its half-century anniversary:

> I want to assure you that if the men who are coming after me will have the same interest, the same thought, and the same Christian spirit that the brothers took they will treat you fairly, treat you honestly. I hope and believe that this institution will be run for time immemorial, and be built to still greater proportions, and show to the world that Studebaker Brothers' will live not only today, but one hundred years hence.

TWENTY-THREE

AND NOW TOMORROW

Like John Mohler fifty years ago, the men who have charge of today's affairs in Studebaker are looking forward, not backward.

To forecast now in its 101st year the future of this enterprise, we must understand that it grows out of historical roots about as old as America's industrial development itself. Today, with the good traditions of a century behind them, the men of Studebaker see that future of their company still interwoven with the growth and development of the nation.

Just as the brothers Studebaker heated their iron and hammered it into wagons, so the character of Studebaker today has been shaped by hard times and good times, panic and depression, reorganization and triumph, until it stands sturdily successful and respected in the tough world of American business enterprise.

Its success grows out of making the decisions and following the policies which proved to be right for American progress as well as for Studebaker. Hindsight now makes many of the old decisions look easy. Take, for example, that moment in 1897 when experimenting with horseless vehicles began. At the time it involved a critical outlay of venture capital. But had the risk not been taken, or had the decision been delayed very long, the company would undoubtedly have accompanied its 5,000 wagon-making competitors into oblivion. Instead, it lived.

Alone, out of all those makers of horse-drawn transportation, Studebaker went on living. And it has survived as an auto-maker while literally hundreds of other companies have failed to do so. For Studebaker, even hard experience and vicissitudes, no less than blessings like California gold for expansion, served a purpose — they taught the need for ingenuity and bold courage. The men of Studebaker today, in planning for tomorrow, draw from that wonderful heritage.

A great tradition is the greatest of all heritages, because it gives men an ideal against which they can measure themselves and their work.

A century of tradition has a value not to be measured in sentiment alone. Neither is it to be measured by the growing financial resources of the organization, nor by its expanding plant capacity at the end of the century. Nor does the increasing number of people it employs and the size of its payroll, nor its volume of sales give to the company its greater significance today, and for the future.

The significance of Studebaker's first century is that in the ideas and ideals of those who today plan for Studebaker's tomorrow, we find a point of view not held by the men of younger companies. The men at South Bend live with a long-range outlook, and they make their plans for long periods of time. Each daily decision and action fit into the picture of Studebaker's future viewed confidently far ahead. Plans are never made on just a day-to-day or year-to-year basis. There is no opportunism. There is complete continuity of effort and purpose.

Thus, confident in the tradition built through a century of trial and success, the men who today have charge of the affairs of Studebaker now see—in the words of Harold S. Vance—"a future much more intriguing than the past . . . a tomorrow that holds unknown but boundless opportunity."

THE END: THE FIRST CENTURY